Indian

The royal kitchens of ancient India developed culinary art with care and expertise and traditional forms of cooking still survive in the country. Indian food gets its characteristic taste and aroma from the country's range of spices. Apart from adding that special quality to food, spices have a medicinal and preservative effect. Turmeric (*haldi*) not only adds colour to the food but also helps in digestion, and asafoetida (*hing*) is an excellent preservative. This book gives recipes for preparing exotic meat dishes and baking rare breads on the tandoor (an oven made of earth and heated by a slow charcoal fire), creating subtly flavoured rice and delicious desserts with *chenna* (curdled milk) and rich cream seasoned with saffron and almonds.

Reshmi Kebab Zafrani

Serves - 4

Minced chicken kebabs on skewers

Preparation time: 1 hour

Cooking time: 10 minutes

INGREDIENTS

Chicken, minced	1 kg / 2.2 lb
Eggs, whisked	2
Cumin powder	2 tsp / 10 gms
Yellow chilli powder	1 tsp / 5 gms
White pepper powder	½ tsp / 3 gms
Salt to taste	
Cashew nut paste	3 tbs / 45 gms / 1½ oz
Ginger paste	4 tsp / 20 gms
Onion paste (pg.iii)	4 tsp / 20 gms
Garam masala (pg.iii)	1 tsp / 5 gms
Saffron (in 2 tbs warm milk)	a pinch
Green coriander, chopped	4 tsp / 20 gms
Processed cheese, grated	½ cup / 100 gms / 3 ½ oz
Oil	4 tsp / 20 ml

METHOD

- Mix the chicken mince along with all the ingredients except oil and keep aside for 30 minutes.
- Shape the chicken mince mixture along the length of skewers to shape into a kebab.
- Cook in a tandoor for 6-8 minutes. Remove from tandoor, baste with oil and cook further for another 5 minutes or until brown.
- Remove from skewers and serve hot.

Aloo Shirazi

Serves - 4

Stuffed potatoes marinated and cooked in a tandoor

Preparation time: 1½ hour
Cooking time: 10 minutes

INGREDIENTS

Potatoes, large	10
For the filling:	
Potatoes, cubed	60 gms / 2 oz
Raisins	60 gms / 2 oz
Cashew nuts, broken	60 gms / 2 oz
Khoya (pg. iii)	60 gms / 2 oz
Almonds, slivered	60 gms / 2 oz

For the Marinade:	
Yoghurt, hung (pg. iii)	½ cup / 100 gms / 3½ oz
Garlic paste (pg. iii)	2 tsp / 10 gms
Ginger paste (pg. iii)	2 tsp / 10 gms
Green chillies, minced	1 tsp / 5 gms
Garam masala	1 tsp / 5 gms
Salt to taste	
Oil (for basting)	1 cup / 200 ml / 7 fl oz
Almonds, roasted	45 gms / 1½ fl oz

METHOD

- Cut the potatoes into barrels and scoop the inside out.
- For the filling, mix together all the ingredients and stuff the hollow potatoes with it.
- For the marinade, mix together all the ingredients and marinate the potatoes in it. Keep aside for 1½ hours.
- Skewer the potatoes and cook in a tandoor for 15-20 minutes. Remove from tandoor, baste with oil and cook again for 5 minutes.
- Remove from skewers and serve hot, garnished with roasted almonds.

Murg Makhmali Kebab

Serves - 4

Creamy chicken kebabs flavoured with processed cheese

Preparation time: 2 hours
Cooking time: 15 minutes

INGREDIENTS

Chicken breast fillets	800 gms / 28 oz
Ginger-garlic paste (pg. iii)	½ cup / 100 gms / 3½ oz
Salt to taste	
Cream	1 cup / 200 gms / 7 oz
Processed cheese	½ cup / 100 gms / 3½ oz
White pepper powder	1 tsp / 5 gms
Green coriander, finely chopped	4 tsp / 20 gms
Green chillies, finely chopped	4 tsp / 20 gms
Mace powder	½ tsp / 3 gms
Nutmeg powder	½ tsp / 3 gms
Eggs, white	3
Butter	4 tbs / 60 gms / 2 oz

METHOD

- Clean the chicken fillets, rub ginger-garlic paste and salt evenly on them and keep aside.
- Mix cream along with processed cheese, white pepper powder, green coriander, green chillies, mace and nutmeg powder and egg white. Coat the fillets evenly with this mixture. Keep aside for 2 hours.
- Skewer the chicken fillets and roast in a moderately hot tandoor for 8-10 minutes, remove, baste with butter and roast again for 3-5 minutes.
- Remove from skewers and serve hot.

Sarson ka Tikka

Serves - 4

Mustard flavoured, roasted chicken cubes

Preparation time: 4 hours

Cooking time: 15-20 minutes

INGREDIENTS

Chicken leg, boneless, cut into pieces	900 gms / 2 lb
Lemon juice	½ cup / 100 ml / 3½ fl oz
Salt to taste	
Ginger-garlic paste (pg. iii)	4 tbs / 60 gms / 2 oz
Green coriander, chopped	½ cup / 100 gms / 3½ oz
Garlic, chopped	5 tbs / 75 gms / 2½ oz
Green chillies, chopped	3 tbs / 45 gms / 1½ oz
Yellow chilli paste	1 tbs / 15 gms
Mustard paste	3 tbs / 45 gms / 1¼ oz
Mustard oil	½ cup / 150 ml / 5 fl oz
Gramflour	4 tbs / 60 gms / 2 oz
Garam masala	2 tsp / 10 gms
Butter	4 tbs / 60 gms / 2 oz

METHOD

- Apply lemon juice, salt to taste and ginger-garlic paste evenly on the chicken pieces.
- Make a paste by blending together green coriander, garlic and green chillies. To this add all the other ingredients except butter.
- Squeeze the chicken pieces and add to the prepared paste. Mix well and keep aside for 3 to 4 hours.
- Skewer the chicken pieces and cook in a tandoor or a charcoal grill for 10 minutes.
- Remove from the tandoor, baste with butter and cook further until done.
- Remove from skewers and serve hot.

Murg Chandni Kebab

Serves - 4

Chicken drumsticks stuffed with chicken mince mixture and cooked in a tandoor

Preparation time: 2 hours

Cooking time: 15 minutes

INGREDIENTS

Chicken, drumsticks	16
Chicken, mince	400 gms / 14 oz
Green cardamom powder	1 tsp / 5 gms
Clove powder	1/3 tsp / 2 gms
Salt to taste	
Ginger-garlic paste (pg. iii)	4 tbs / 60 gms / 2 oz
White pepper powder	½ tsp / 3 gms
Eggs, whisked	1
Cheese, grated	½ cup / 100 gms / 3½ oz
Green chillies, chopped	5 tsp / 25 gms
Green coriander, chopped	4 tsp / 20 gms
Cream	1 cup / 200 gms / 7 oz
Nutmeg & Mace powder	½ tsp / 3 gms
Butter (for basting)	½ cup / 100 gms / 3½ oz
Silver foil	

METHOD

- Debone the chicken drumsticks and keep aside.
- Mix the chicken mince along with green cardamom powder, clove powder and salt. Fill the drumsticks with the mixture and seal with a toothpick.
- Make a marinade with the remaining ingredients except butter and silver foil and marinate the chicken drumsticks in it. Keep aside for 2 hours.
- Skewer the drumsticks and cook in a tandoor for 10 minutes. Remove from tandoor, baste with butter and cook for another 2-5 minutes.
- Remove from skewers, remove the toothpick. Wrap silver foil over a third of the drumsticks and serve.

Tangri Kebab Haryali

Serves - 4

Mint and coriander flavoured kebabs

Preparation time: 3 hours

Cooking time: 15 minutes

INGREDIENTS

Chicken, legs	12
Ginger paste (pg. iii)	4 tsp / 20 gms
Garlic paste (pg. iii)	1 tbs / 15 gms
Salt to taste	
Lemon juice	1 tbs / 15 ml
Yoghurt, hung (pg. iii)	½ cup / 100 gms / 3½ oz
Mint, finely chopped	2 tbs / 30 gms / 1 oz
Green coriander, chopped	¼ cup / 50 gms / 1¾ oz
Garam masala	1 tsp / 5 gms
Coriander powder	1 tsp / 5 gms
Cumin powder	1 tsp / 5 gms
Oil	4 tbs / 60 ml / 2 fl oz
Dry fenugreek	1 tsp / 5 gms
Green chillies, finely chopped	1 tbs / 15 gms
Butter for basting	

METHOD

- Marinate the chicken legs with ginger paste, garlic paste, salt to taste and lemon juice. Keep aside for 30 minutes.
- Mix all the other ingredients and marinate the chicken legs with the prepared mixture. Keep aside for 2½ hours.
- Skewer the chicken legs and cook in a tandoor for 8-10 minutes.
- Remove from tandoor, baste with butter and cook further for 5 minutes or until done.
- Remove from skewers and serve hot.

Badam ke Shammi Kebab

Serves - 4

Minced lamb kebabs flavoured with almonds

Preparation time: 1 hour

Cooking time: 20 minutes

INGREDIENTS

Lamb, minced	1 kg / 2.2 lb
Lentils	2 tbs / 30 gms / 1 oz
Red chillies, whole	5
Green chillies, whole	5
Black cardamoms	5
Bay leaves	5
Cinnamon sticks	5
Cloves	10
Water	10 cups / 2 litres / 64 fl oz
Eggs	3
Salt	2 tsp / 10 gms
Almonds, slivered	2 oz / 60 gms
Oil for frying	

METHOD

- Boil the mince along with lentils, red chillies, green chillies and all the whole spices in water till all the water evaporates.
- Remove the whole spices from the mince and discard them. Mash the mince well.
- Add eggs and salt to mixture and knead it well. Sprinkle almonds and mix well.
- Divide the mixture into even sized balls and shape into cutlets.
- Heat oil in a wok and deep fry the cutlets until crisp and brown on all sides.
- Remove, drain excess oil and serve hot.

Paneer Sabut Dane ka Kebab

Serves - 4

Cottage cheese and sago croquettes

Preparation time: 1 hour

Cooking time: 15 minutes

INGREDIENTS

Cottage cheese (*paneer*)	500 gms / 1.1 lb
Sago	100 gms / 3½ oz
Spring onions, minced	100 gms / 3½ oz
Green chillies, chopped	2 tsp / 10 gms
Cashew nuts, broken	45 gms / 1½ oz
Raisins (sultanas)	60 gms / 2 oz
Cumin seeds, roasted	1 tsp / 5 gms
Turmeric powder	½ tsp / 3 gms
Garam masala	1 tsp / 5 gms
Cornflour	2 tbs / 30 gms / 1 oz
Salt to taste	
Oil for frying	

METHOD

- Mash the cottage cheese and heat it so that it leaves water. Squeeze and mash again.
- Boil sago pellets and drain. Blend to break into smaller lumps without making it into a paste.
- Mix together all the ingredients along with mashed cottage cheese and sago paste and knead. Keep aside for ½ hour.
- Shape into flat round cutlets. Heat a griddle, brush with oil and fry the cutlets a few at a time until golden brown in colour.
- Remove, drain excess oil and serve hot.

Bharwan Shimla Mirch

Serves - 4

Stuffed capsicum

Preparation time: 30 minutes

Cooking time: 45 minutes

INGREDIENTS

Capsicum	600 gms / 22 oz
Oil	4 tbs / 60 ml / 2 fl oz
Ginger, chopped	15 gms
Cumin seeds	2 tsp / 10 gms
Potatoes, boiled, cut into dices	100 gms / 3½ oz
Cottage cheese (*paneer*)	100 gms / 3½ oz
Red chilli powder	1 tbs / 15 gms
Turmeric powder	2 tbs / 10 gms
Garam masala	1 tsp / 5 gms
Cumin powder	1 tbs / 15 gms
Cashew nuts	45 gms / 1½ oz
Raisins	25 gms
Green chillies, chopped	1 tbs / 15 gms
Green Coriander, chopped	1 tbs / 15 gms
Salt to taste	
For the Marinade:	
Yoghurt, hung (pg iii)	1 cup / 200 gms / 7 oz
Red chilli paste	4 tsp / 20 gms
Ginger-garlic paste (pg. iii)	4 tsp / 20 gms
Garam masala	½ tsp / 3 gms
Salt to taste	
Butter for basting	
Cumin powder	½ tsp / 3 gms

METHOD

- Remove top of capsicums and scoop out seeds. Keep top aside.
- Heat oil in a wok, add ginger and cumin seeds, sauté till they crackle, add potatoes and cottage cheese. Sauté for a few minutes. Stir in dry spices along with the remaining ingredients. Mix well and remove from heat.
- Fill the capsicums with this mixture and cover with top.
- For the marinade, mix all the ingredients and coat the capsicums with it.
- Skewer the capsicums and cook in a tandoor for 10 minutes, Remove, baste with butter and cook further for 2-5 minutes. Serve hot.

Kebab-e-Chaman

Serves - 4

Spinach and potato cutlets

Preparation time: 1 hour

Cooking time: 15 minutes

INGREDIENTS

Spinach	1 kg / 2.2 lb
Potatoes	400 gms / 14 oz
Lentils	¾ cup / 150 gms / 5 oz
Green chillies	5 tsp / 25 gms
Ginger	5 tsp / 25 gms
Green coriander	5 tsp / 25 gms
Raisins, finely chopped	½ cup / 100 gms / 3½ oz
Cumin powder	4 tsp / 20 gms
Coriander powder	1 tsp / 15 gms
Dry fenugreek powder	2 tsp / 10 gms
Garam masala	2 tsp / 10 gms
Cashew nut, chopped	½ cup / 100 gms /3½ oz
Salt to taste	
Clarified butter	¾ cup / 150 gms / 5 oz

METHOD

- Boil the spinach, potatoes and lentils separately.
- Chop the spinach finely, mash the potatoes and lentils.
- Chop green chillies, ginger and green coriander finely and mix into the mashed potatoes and lentils alongwith spinach and all the other ingredients except clarified butter.
- Shape into flat round cutlets.
- Heat a griddle and shallow fry the cutlets in clarified butter until crisp and golden brown on both sides.
- Remove, drain excess clarified butter and serve hot.

Seekh Kebab Gilafi

Serves - 4

An exotic and colourful Kebab

Preparation time: 2 hours

Cooking time: 15 minutes

INGREDIENTS

Lamb, minced	1 kg / 2.2 lb
Ginger paste (pg. iii)	3 tbs / 45 gms / 1½ oz
Onion paste, browned (pg. iii)	1¼ cup / 240 gms / 9 oz
Green chillies, minced	6
Garam masala	2 tsp / 10 gms
Red chilli powder	2 tsp / 10 gms
Salt	2 tsp / 10 gms
Oil	3 tbs / 45 ml / 1½ fl oz
Processed cheese	½ cup / 100 gms / 3½ oz
Onions, finely chopped	100 gms / 3½ oz
Capsicum, chopped	100 gms / 3½ oz
Tomatoes, deseeded & finely chopped	100 gms / 3½ oz
Butter for basting	

METHOD

- Mix the lamb mince along with ginger paste, brown onion paste, green chillies, garam masala, red chilli powder, salt, oil and processed cheese.
- Mix together onions, capsicum and tomatoes.
- Squeeze out excess water, if any from the mince mixture and mix thoroughly. Keep aside for 2 hours.
- Shape the mince mixture along the length of skewers and coat with the onion mixture.
- Roast in a tandoor for 10-15 minutes, basting with butter at regular intervals. Remove from skewers and serve hot.

Aloo Lajawab

Serves - 4

Stir-fried potatoes

Preparation time: 40 minutes

Cooking time: 30 minutes

INGREDIENTS

Potatoes, boiled	1 kg / 2.2 lb
Clarified butter / Oil	½ cup / 100 gms / 3½ oz
Cumin seeds	5 tsp / 25 gms
Chaat masala	3 tsp / 45 gms / 1½ oz
Cumin powder	5 tsp / 25 gms
Turmeric powder	1 tsp / 15 gms
Mint leaves, chopped	5 tbs / 75 gms / 2½ oz
Dry fenugreek	5 tsp / 25 gms
Garam masala	4 tsp / 20 gms
Salt to taste	
Coriander powder	2 tbs / 30 gms / 1 oz
Green chillies, chopped	5 tsp / 25 gms
Green coriander, chopped	2 tbs / 30 gms / 1 oz
Butter	2 tbs / 30 gms / 1 oz

METHOD

- Cut the boiled potatoes into dices.
- Heat clarified butter / oil in a pan, add cumin seeds and sauté till they crackle. Add the diced potatoes and stir-fry for a minute.
- Stir in chaat masala, cumin powder, turmeric powder, mint leaves, dry fenugreek powder, garam masala, salt to taste and coriander powder.
- Add the green chillies and green coriander. Cover and cook for 2-3 minutes.
- Stir in butter and remove from heat. Serve hot.

Bharwan Karela

Serves - 4

Stuffed bitter gourds

Preparation time: 1 hour

Cooking time: 45 minutes

INGREDIENTS

Bitter gourds	1 kg / 2.2 lb
Mustard oil for frying	
Mustard oil	3 tbs / 45 ml / 1½ fl oz
Yoghurt (pg. iii)	½ cup / 100 gms / 3½ oz
Salt to taste	
Red chilli powder	1 tsp / 5 gms
Ginger paste (pg. iii)	1 tsp / 5 gms
For the filling:	
Clarified butter	4 tbs / 60 gms / 2 oz
Asafoetida powder	a pinch
Sugar	2 tsp / 10 gms
Salt	2 tsp / 10 gms
Potatoes, cut into ½" cubes	120 gms / 4 oz
Cumin	½ tsp / 3 gms
Lentils, boiled & drained	120 gms / 4 oz
Tamarind pulp	2 tsp / 10 gms
Fennel	2 tsp / 10 gms
Red chilli powder	1 tsp / 5 gms
Onion paste (pg. iii)	4 tbs / 60 gms / 2 oz
Garlic paste (pg. iii)	2 tsp / 10 gms
Ginger, chopped	2 tsp / 10 gms
Green chillies, chopped	2 tsp / 10 gms
Green coriander, chopped	1 tsp / 5 gms
Water	½ cup / 100 ml / 3½ fl oz

METHOD

- Scrape the bitter gourds and boil them in water till half cooked. Slit, remove seeds and squeeze them gently to remove water.
- Heat mustard oil in a wok, deep fry till crisp. Remove, keep aside.
- For th filling. heat clarified butter in a pan, add asafoetida alongwith all the other ingredients. Stir-fry for a few minutes, add water and cook till the water evaporates. Remove from heat.
- Stuff the bitter gourds with the mixture and tie with a thread.
- In a separate pan, heat mustard oil (3 tbs), add all the other ingredients along with the bitter gourds and cook till moisture evaporates. Remove and serve hot.

Paneer Tawa Masala

Serves - 4

Stir-fried cottage cheese cooked on a griddle

Preparation time: 20 minutes

Cooking time: 30 minutes

INGREDIENTS

Cottage cheese (*paneer*), cut into cubes	700 gms / 25 oz
Clarified butter	½ cup / 100 gms / 3½ oz
Carom seeds	1 tsp / 5 gms
Onions, chopped	1 cup / 200 gms / 7 oz
Ginger, chopped	1 tbs / 15 gms
Green chillies, chopped	5
Red chilli powder	1 tsp / 5 gms
Coriander powder	1 tsp / 5 gms
Makhni gravy (pg. 37)	1¼ cup / 250 ml / 9 oz
Salt to taste	
Garam masala	1 tsp / 5 gms
Green coriander, chopped	2 tsp / 10 gms

METHOD

- Heat clarified butter in a griddle, add carom seeds and sauté till they crackle. Add onions, ginger, green chillies and sauté for 5 minutes.
- Stir in red chilli powder and coriander powder alongwith cottage cheese cubes and stir for a minute to cook.
- Stir in the *makhni* gravy, cover and cook till it thickens and the cottage cheese cubes are coated with it.
- Check seasoning, add garam masala and green coriander. Mix well and remove from heat. Serve hot.

Mirch aur Baigan ka Salan

Serves - 4

A hot curry made from green chillies and aubergines

Preparation time: 30 minutes
Cooking time: 30 minutes

INGREDIENTS

Green chillies, large	100 gms / 3½ oz
Aubergines, small	250 gms / 9 oz
Oil for frying	2½ cups / 500 ml / 16 fl oz
For the gravy:	
Onions, sliced	4 tbs / 60 gms / 2 oz
Groundnuts	45 gms / 1½ oz
Sesame seeds	5 tsp / 25 gms
Coconut, dry, grated	5 tsp / 25 gms
Yoghurt (pg. iii)	1 cup / 200 gms / 7 oz
Oil	½ cup / 100 ml / 3½ fl oz
Mustard seeds	½ tsp / 3 gms
Fenugreek seeds	½ tsp / 3 gms
Onion seeds	½ tsp / 3 gms
Red chillies, whole	5
Curry leaves	½ tsp / 3 gms
Turmeric powder	½ tsp / 3 gms
Cumin powder	½ tsp / 3 gms
Coriander powder	½ tsp / 3 gms
Dry fenugreek powder	½ tsp / 3 gms
Tamarind	3 tbs / 45 gms / 1½ oz
Ginger-garlic paste (pg. iii)	3 tbs / 45 gms / 1½ oz

METHOD

- Slit the green chillies and aubergines. Heat oil in a pan and deep fry the green chillies and aubergines. Drain excess oil and keep aside.
- For the gravy, deep fry the onions in the same oil and keep aside. Broil the groundnut, sesame seeds and coconut. Blend them alongwith fried onions and yoghurt to make a paste. Keep aside.
- Heat oil in a wok, add mustard seeds, fenugreek seeds, onions seeds and the prepared paste alongwith all the ingredients. Cook till it leaves oil.
- Add the fried green chillies and aubergines to it. Reduce heat to low and cook for a few minutes.
- Remove from heat and serve hot.

Daal Kandahari

Serves - 4

Lentil curry

Preparation time: 20 minutes

Cooking time: 1 hour

INGREDIENTS

Lentils (*urad daal*)	120 gms / 4 oz
Water	7½ cups / 1.5 litres
Salt to taste	
Ginger-garlic paste (pg. iii)	3 tbs / 45 gms / 1½ oz
Tomato purée (pg. iii)	½ cup / 120 ml / 4 fl oz
Red chilli paste (pg. iii)	5 tsp / 25 gms
White butter	½ cup / 120 gms / 4 oz
Cream	½ cup / 100 gms / 3½ oz
Green coriander, chopped	2 tsp / 10 gms

METHOD

- Boil the soaked lentils in water along with salt to taste until the lentils are tender and the water has reduced to ¼.
- Stir in ginger-garlic paste, tomato purée, red chilli paste, white butter and cream. Mix well and cook for about 45 minutes on very low heat.
- Adjust seasoning and cook further for 5 minutes.
- Remove from heat onto a serving bowl, drizzle cream on top and garnish with green coriander. Serve hot.

Tandoori Murg

Serves - 4

Tandoori chicken

Preparation time: 2 hours

Cooking time: 15 minutes

INGREDIENTS

Chicken, cut into big pieces	2 (600 gms each) / 22 oz
Red chilli powder	2 tsp / 10 gms
Salt to taste	
Lemon juice	4 tbs / 60 ml / 2 fl oz
Yoghurt (pg. iii)	¾ cup / 150 gms / 5 oz
Oil	½ cup / 100 ml / 3½ fl oz
Ginger-Garlic paste (pg. iii)	2 tbs / 30 gms / 1 oz
Cumin (jeera) powder	2 tsp / 10 gms
Garam masala	4 tbs / 60 gms / 2 oz
Butter	4 tbs / 60 gms / 2 oz

METHOD

- Clean the chicken and make incisions on the skin.
- Prepare a marinade by mixing together red chilli powder, salt to taste, lemon juice and rub evenly over the chicken. Keep aside for 2 hours.
- Whisk yoghurt along with oil, ginger-garlic paste, cumin powder, garam masala and rub on the chicken.
- Skewer the chicken and roast in a moderately hot tandoor for 8-10 minutes.
- Remove from tandoor, baste with butter and roast again for 3-4 minutes.
- Remove from skewers and serve hot, accompanied by mint chuntney.

Murg Mumtaz

Serves - 4

Chicken cooked in tomato gravy

Preparation time: 2 hours

Cooking time: 45 minutes

INGREDIENTS

Chicken, cut into boneless pieces	1 kg / 2.2 lb
Salt to taste	
Ginger-garlic paste (pg. iii)	4 tsp / 20 gms
Lemon juice	2 tbs / 30 ml
For the Marinade:	
Yoghurt, hung (pg. iii)	½ cup / 100 gms / 3½ oz
Garlic paste (pg. iii)	2 tsp / 10 gms
Cumin powder	1 tbs / 15 gms
Red chilli paste (pg. iii)	1 tbs / 30 gms / 1 oz
Oil	5 tbs / 75 ml / 2½ oz
Salt to taste	

***Makhni* Gravy:**	
Tomatoes	1 kg / 2.2 lb
Ginger-garlic paste (pg. iii)	2 tbs / 30 gms / 1 oz
Green chillies	10
Red chilli powder	1 tsp / 5 gms
Cloves powder	1 tsp / 5 gms
Green cardamom powder	1 tsp / 5 gms
Butter	1 cup / 200 gms / 7 oz
Cream	¾ cup / 150 gms / 5 oz
Dry fenugreek powder	2 tsp / 10 gms
Garam masala	1 tsp / 5 gms
Water	2½ cups / 500 ml / 16 fl oz
Salt to taste	

METHOD

- Rub salt, ginger-garlic paste and lemon juice on the chicken pieces. Keep aside for 20 minutes.
- Prepare a marinade with all the ingredients and coat the chicken pieces with it. Keep aside for 2 hours.
- For the *makhni* gravy, heat a pot, add all the ingredients in it except butter, cream, dry fenugreek powder and garam masala. Cook for 30 minutes mashing continuously.
- Strain and return to heat. Cook till the gravy thickens, add remaining ingredients. Cook for 5 minutes and remove from heat.
- Skewer the chicken pieces and cook in a tandoor for 10 minutes and add to the gravy. Mix well and serve.

Sarson ka Murg

Serves - 4

Chicken flavoured with mustard

Preparation time: 20 minutes

Cooking time: 1 hour

INGREDIENTS

Chicken, cut into 4 pieces	1 kg / 2.2 lb
Ginger paste (pg. iii)	3 tbs / 45 gms / 1½ oz
Garlic paste (pg. iii)	5 tsp / 25 gms
Mustard oil	5 tbs / 75 ml / 2½ fl oz
Mustard seeds	1 tsp / 5 gms
Fenugreek seeds	1 tsp / 5 gms
Red chilli paste	1 tbs / 15 gms
Salt to taste	
Cumin powder	1 tsp / 5 gms
Coriander powder	1 tsp / 5 gms
Garam masala	1 tsp / 5 gms
Mustard powder	2 tsp / 10 gms
Mint leaves, chopped	3 tbs / 45 gms / 1½ oz
Green coriander, chopped	½ cup / 100 gms / 3½ oz
Green chillies, chopped	3 tbs / 45 gms / 1½ oz
Tomatoes, chopped	½ cup / 100 gms / 3½ oz

METHOD

- Apply half of ginger paste, garlic paste along with salt on the pieces and keep aside.
- Heat mustard oil in a pan, add mustard seeds, fenugreek seeds, sauté till they crackle.
- Add red chilli paste, remaining ginger paste, garlic paste, salt to taste, cumin powder, coriander powder, garam masala and mustard powder. Mix well.
- Prepare a paste by blending together mint, coriander and green chillies and add to the pan.
- Add the chicken pieces to the gravy and cook till the oil separates.
- Add a little water and cook on low heat for 15-20 minutes or till done.
- Remove from heat and serve hot, garnished with chopped tomatoes.

Kandhari Pulao

Serves - 4

Fragrant rice

Preparation time: 40 minutes

Cooking time: 1 hour

INGREDIENTS

Basmati rice	1½ cup / 300 gms / 11 oz	Walnuts, fried	60 gms / 2 oz
Clarified butter	1 cup / 200 gms / 7 oz	Almonds, fried	60 gms / 2 oz
Garam masala, whole	2 tsp / 10 gms	Peanuts, fried	60 gms / 2 oz
Water	2¼ cup / 450 ml / 15 fl oz	Pistachios, fried	60 gms / 2 oz
Saffron	½ tsp / 3 gms	Raisins, fried	60 gms / 2 oz
Warm milk	½ cup / 100 ml / 3½ fl oz	Rose water	1 tbs / 15 ml
Cashew nuts, broken, fried	60 gms / 2 oz	Onions, fried	½ cup / 100 gms / 3½ cup

METHOD

- Soak rice in sufficient water for 30 minutes. Drain and keep aside.
- Heat clarified butter in a pan and add the whole garam masala. Sauté till they crackle.
- Add the rice and fry till a pleasing smell emanates. Add water (2¼ cup) and boil till ¾ done. Drain and keep aside. Soak saffron in warm milk.
- In a pot, sprinkle some saffron mixture, spread a layer of rice and dry fruits, then sprinkle the remaining saffron mixture, rose water and fried onions. Seal the pot with aluminum foil.
- Cook on very low heat for 30 minutes. Remove from heat and serve hot.

Chicken Biryani

Serves - 4

Rice dish cooked on a slow fire with chicken and spices

Preparation time: 1 hour
Cooking time: 30 minutes

INGREDIENTS

Chicken, cut into pieces	1 kg / 2.2 lb
Basmati rice	1 kg / 2.2 lb
Yoghurt (pg. iii)	1½ cup / 300 gms / 11 oz
Ginger-garlic paste (pg. iii)	3 tbs / 45 gms / 1½ oz
Salt to taste	
Yellow chilli powder	1 tbs / 15 gms
Garam masala	1 tsp / 5 gms
Clarified butter	1¼ cups / 250 gms / 9 oz
Garam masala, whole	4 tsp / 20 gms
Onions, sliced	250 gms + 200 gms
Mint, chopped	4 tsp / 20 gms
Green coriander, chopped	2 tbs / 30 gms / 1 oz
Saffron	½ tsp / 3 gms
Milk	½ cup / 100 ml / 3½ fl oz
Chicken stock	20 cups / 4 litres

METHOD

- Marinate the chicken pieces with yoghurt, ginger-garlic paste, salt to taste, yellow chilli powder and garam masala.
- Heat clarified butter (¾ cup) in a pot, add whole garam masala and onions. Sauté till golden brown. Add the chicken pieces without marinade and stir-fry till water evaporates.
- Stir in the marinade, mint and green coriander. Cook on low heat till the chicken pieces are tender.
- Make a mixture of saffron, clarified butter (½ cup) and milk (½ cup) and keep warm. Boil rice in chicken stock.
- In a pot, arrange alternate layers of rice, chicken pieces, saffron mixture and fried onions.
- Cover the pot with a wet cloth. Seal with lid and dough. Bake in a moderately hot oven for 15 minutes. Remove and serve hot.

Mutton Biryani

Serves - 4

Rice dish cooked on a slow fire with mutton and spices

Preparation time: 30 minutes

Cooking time:1 hour

INGREDIENTS

Mutton, cut into pieces	600 gms / 22 oz
Rice	1½ cups / 300 gms / 11 oz
Clarified butter	¾ cup / 150 gms / 5 oz
Yoghurt (pg. iii)	1 cup / 200 gms / 7 oz
Red chilli powder	1 tbs / 15 gms
Ginger paste (pg. iii)	1 tbs / 15 gms
Asafoetida powder	1 tsp / 5 gms
Cumin powder	½ tsp / 3 gms
Cloves powder	½ tsp / 3 gms
Black cardamom powder	½ tsp / 3 gms
Vetivier water	4 tsp / 20 ml
Saffron	½ tsp / 3 gms
Milk	1 cup / 200 ml / 7 fl oz

METHOD

- Heat clarified butter in a pan, add the mutton pieces and sauté till light brown. Add yoghurt, red chilli powder, ginger paste and asafoetida powder. Cook on low heat till the meat pieces are tender.
- Stir in the remaining spices except vetivier water, saffron and milk.
- Boil rice in sufficient water. Drain excess water and keep aside. Soak saffron in milk (1 cup).
- In a greased, heavy bottomed pan, sprinkle half of rice, vetivier water, saffron milk and mutton pieces. Repeat the same process till all rice, vetivier water, saffron milk and mutton pieces are used.
- Cover and seal the pan, cook on very low heat for 30 minutes. Remove and serve hot.

Naan

Serves - 4

Leavened bread

Preparation time: 2 hours

Cooking time: 5-10 minutes

INGREDIENTS

Refined flour	2½ cup / 500 gms / 1.1 lb
Soda-bi-carb	a pinch
Salt to taste	
Baking powder	1 tsp / 5 gms
Egg	1
Sugar	2 tsp / 10 gms
Yoghurt (pg. iii)	5 tsp / 25 gms
Milk	4 tsp / 20 ml
Water as required	
Oil	2 tbs / 30 ml / 1 fl oz
Melon seeds	1 tsp / 5 gms
Onion seeds	1 tsp / 5 gms

METHOD

- Sieve the flour along with salt, soda-bi-carb & baking powder in a mixing bowl.
- Add egg, sugar, yoghurt and milk along with water and knead to a smooth soft dough. Cover with a moist cloth and keep aside for 10 minutes.
- Add oil to the dough and knead further. Cover with a moist cloth and keep aside for 2 hours.
- Divide the dough into equal portions and shape into balls. Flatten the balls between palms to an oval shape. Sprinkle melon and onion seeds.
- Cook in a tandoor till light brown spots appear on the surface.
- Remove and serve hot, as an accompaniment to any meal.

Pudina Parantha

Serves - 4

Whole wheat bread flavoured with mint

Preparation time: 30 minutes

Cooking time: 10 minutes

INGREDIENTS

Whole wheat flour	2½ cups / 500 gms / 1.1 lb
Salt	1 tsp / 5 gms
Clarified butter	½ cup / 120 gms / 3½ oz
Water	1¼ cups / 250 ml / 8 fl oz
Mint leaves, dried	1 tsp / 5 gms

METHOD

- In a mixing bowl, mix flour with salt and half of clarified butter, add water and knead to a smooth dough. Cover and keep aside for 30 minutes.
- Shape the dough into a ball and flatten into a round disc using a rolling pin. Apply the remaining clarified butter and sprinkle dried mint leaves.
- Pleat the dough into 1 collected strip. Shape into balls and roll out into a 6" diameter pancake. Repeat the same process with the remaining balls.
- Heat a griddle / tandoor and cook till brown spots appear on both the sides.
- Remove from griddle / tandoor and serve hot.

Missi Roti

Serves - 4

Flavoured gramflour bread cooked in a tandoor

Preparation time: 30 minutes

Cooking time: 10 minutes

INGREDIENTS

Gramflour	1½ cups / 300 gms / 11 oz
Flour	½ cup / 100 gms / 3½ oz
Green chillies, chopped	5 tsp / 25 gms
Ginger, chopped	5 tsp / 25 gms
Green coriander, chopped	5 tp / 25 gms
Pomegranate seeds	4 tsp / 20 gms
Cumin seeds	1 tbs / 15 gms
Salt	2 tbs / 10 gms
Onion seeds	5 tsp / 25 gms
Water as required	
Clarified butter	1 tbs / 30 gms / 1 oz
Butter	½ cup / 100 gms / 3½ oz

METHOD

- Chop the green chillies, ginger and green coriander finely.
- Crush the pomegranate seeds, cumin seeds and onion seeds with a rolling pin.
- Mix together gramflour and flour along with all the other ingredients except butter and knead to smooth soft dough using water.
- Shape into even sized balls and roll out into 6" diameter pancake.
- Cook in a tandoor/griddle until brown on both sides.
- Remove from tandoor/griddle, apply butter and serve hot.

Chenna Payas

Serves - 4

Chenna dumplings in flavoured milk

Preparation time: 1 hour

Cooking time: 1 hour

INGREDIENTS

Chenna (pg. iii)	½ cup / 100 gms / 3½ oz
Refined flour	1 tsp / 5 gms
Baking powder	a pinch
Water	¾ cup / 150 ml / 5 fl oz
Sugar	1 cup / 250 gms / 9 oz

For the *payas*:

Milk	10 cups / 2 litres
Sugar	1 cup / 250 gms / 9 oz
Vetivier essence	a few drops
Pistachios, slivered	10 gms

METHOD

- Mash the *chenna* and mix in flour and baking powder.
- For the sugar syrup, boil water in a pan, add sugar and stir till it reaches a thread-like consistency. Reduce heat to low.
- Make small balls from the *chenna* and poach in sugar syrup till they float on top. Allow to cool.
- For the *payas*, heat milk in a pan till it reduces to half. Mix in all the other ingredients and remove from heat.
- Squeeze the sugar syrup from the balls and dip into the prepared payas.
- Chill in a refrigerator and serve cold.

Phirni

Serves - 4

Richly garnished rice pudding

Preparation time: 30 minutes

Cooking time: 30 minutes

INGREDIENTS

Basmati rice	4 tbs / 60 gms / 2 oz
Saffron	a few strands
Milk	5 cups / 1 litre
Sugar	1 cup / 250 gms / 9 oz
Green cardamom powder	1 tsp / 5 gms
Rose water	2 drops
Almonds, slivered	10 gms
Pistachios, slivered	5 gms
Silver leaves for garnish	

METHOD

- Soak the rice in sufficient water for 30 minutes. Drain and blend to a smooth paste. Soak saffron in 1 tbs of warm milk.
- Heat a thick bottomed pan, add milk and bring to a boil, stir in the rice paste and sugar, cook till the mixture thickens.
- Add saffron soaked in warm milk, green cardamom powder and rose water. Mix well and remove from heat.
- Allow to cool and chill in a refrigerator.
- Serve chilled, garnished with almonds, pistachios and silver leaves.

Gulab Jamun

Serves - 4

Dried milk dumplings, deep fried and soaked in sugar syrup

Preparation time: 1 hour

Cooking time: 30 minutes

INGREDIENTS

Khoya (pg. iii)	1½ cups / 300 gms / 11 oz
Chenna (pg. iii)	4 tbs / 60 gms / 2 oz
Refined flour	3 tbs / 45 gms / 1½ oz
Soda-bi-carb	a pinch
Water	14 cups / 2.7 litres
Sugar	3¾ cups / 900 gms / 2 lb
Green cardamom powder	2 tsp / 10 gms
Pistachios, chopped	10 gms
Saffron	a pinch
Rose water	2 drops
Clarified butter for deep frying	

METHOD

- Mash *khoya* and *chenna* gently to break all granules.
- Add refined flour, soda-bi-carb and knead gently. Keep some of the *chenna* mixture aside and make small balls with the remaining mixture.
- Prepare the sugar syrup by boiling water along with sugar till it reaches a thread-like consistency. Reduce heat to low.
- Take the mixture kept aside and mix green cardamon powder, pistachios, saffron strands and rose water.
- Stuff this mixture in the prepared balls.
- Heat clarified butter in a wok and deep fry the prepared balls over medium heat until golden brown.
- Remove, drain excess oil and immerse directly into the sugar syrup. Serve hot.

Ras Malai

Serves - 4

Sweet medallions in saffron flavoured milk

Preparation time: 1 hour

Cooking time: 45 minutes

INGREDIENTS

Chenna (pg. iii)	1¼ cup / 250 gms / 9 oz
Rabari (unsweetened)	2½ cups / 500 gms / 1.1 lb
Sugar	3 cups / 750 gms / 26 oz
Refined flour	1 tbs / 15 gms
Baking powder	½ tsp / 3 gms
Water	2 cups / 400 ml / 14 fl oz
Pistachios, slivered	5 gms

METHOD

- Heat the *rabari* in a thick bottomed pan to thin it down. Stir in sugar (¾ cup) and mix well. Remove from heat, allow to cool and chill in a refrigerator.
- Knead the *chenna* with flour and baking powder and shape into balls. Gently flatten the balls in between palms to shape into patties.
- Prepare the sugar syrup by boiling the remaining sugar along with water till it reaches a thread-like consistency. Reduce heat to low.
- Poach the patties in the sugar syrup till light and fluffy.
- Squeeze the patties to drain excess sugar syrup and add to the prepared *rabari*.
- Garnish with pistachios and serve cold.

Pista Kulfi

Serves - 4

Rich and flavourful homemade ice cream

Preparation time: 12 hours

Cooking time: 30 minutes

INGREDIENTS

Rabari (unsweetened)	1 kg / 2.2 lb
Saffron	½ tsp / 3 gms
Warm milk	2 tbs / 30 ml / 1 fl oz
Sugar	1⅔ cups / 400 gms / 14 oz
Pistachios, crushed	½ cup / 100 gms / 3½ oz
Green cardamom, crushed	½ tsp / 3 gms
Falooda for garnishing	
Rose syrup for garnishing	

METHOD

- Soak saffron in warm milk. Heat a thick bottomed pan, add *rabari* and cook till it dries up a little.
- Add the soaked saffron to the *rabari*, mix well and remove from heat.
- Stir in sugar, pistachios and green cardamom and mix well.
- Fill the mixture in *kulfi* moulds and freeze in a refrigerator for 12 hours.
- Remove the *kulfi* moulds from the refrigerator and serve, garnished with *falooda* and rose syrup.

Malpua Rabari

Serves - 4

Shallow fried pancakes, soaked in sugar syrup and served with flavoured milk

Preparation time: 1 hour 30 minutes
Cooking time: 1 hour

INGREDIENTS

Refined flour	1¼ cups / 250 gms / 9 oz
Water (for sugar syrup)	1¼ cups / 250 gms / 8 fl oz
Sugar	1¼ cups / 250 gms / 9 oz
Baking powder	½ tsp / 3 gms
Yoghurt (pg. iii)	½ cup / 120 gms / 4 oz
Green cardamom powder	1 tsp / 5 gms
Saffron soaked in 1 tbs milk	½ tsp / 3 gms
Clarified butter	1¼ cups / 250 gms / 9 oz

For the *Rabari*:

Milk	15 cups / 3 litres
Sugar	$1^1/_3$ cups/ 350 gms / 12 oz
Rose water	5 drops
Pistachios, chopped	20 gms

METHOD

- For the sugar syrup, heat water in a pan, add sugar and cook till it reaches a thread-like consistency. Reduce heat.
- Sieve flour and baking powder in a mixing bowl. Add all the other ingredients except clarified butter to make a batter of pouring consistency with water. Add milk if required.
- Heat clarified butter in a flat pan, drop spoonfuls of batter in it and fry on both sides till golden brown.
- Dip the fried *malpuas* in sugar syrup and remove immediately.
- For the *rabari*, heat, milk in a thick bottomed wok till it reduces to $^1/_3$. Stir in the remaining ingredients and remove from heat.
- Allow to cool and refrigerate. Serve with the prepared malpuas.

Raj Bhog

Serves - 4

Chenna dumplings stuffed with pistachios, dipped in sugar syrup

Preparation time: 30 minutes
Cooking time: 1 hour

INGREDIENTS

Chenna (pg. iii)	1¼ cups / 250 gms / 9 oz	Sugar candy	6
Refined flour	2 tsp / 10 gms	Sugar	2½ cups / 600 gms / 22 oz
Orange colour	1 drop	Pistachios, chopped	5 gms
Baking powder	½ tsp / 3 gms	Saffron	a few strands
Water	10 cups / 2 litres		

METHOD

- Mash the *chenna*, flour, orange colour and baking powder together and mix well.
- Shape into 3" balls and stuff each ball with a candy sugar, pistachios and 2-3 strands of saffron.
- Prepare the sugar syrup by boiling water alongwith sugar till it reaches a thread-like consistency.
- Poach the balls in sugar syrup until they become light and float on the surface acquiring a spongy texture.
- Chill along with the sugar syrup in a refrigerator and serve cold.

Chinese

The term Chinese cuisine conjures up an image of delicately flavoured soups, hot spicy chicken drumsticks, giant-sized lobsters served with exotic-sounding sauces, rice and noodles which are meals in themselves. Chinese food has various schools which have developed from the many civilizations which inhabited different regions of China at different historical periods. The Honan school is famous for its sweet and sour dishes and rich seasonings, the Cantonese school developed the art of sauté cooking in the Chinese wok and roasting and grilling and the Cantons gave the world the fried rice. The Szechaun school is known for its hot and spicy food; chicken with black pepper and the Szechaun duck are permanent favourites all over the world.

Crabmeat Seafood Soup

Serves - 4

Preparation time: 10 minutes

Cooking time: 5 minutes

INGREDIENTS

Chicken stock	2¼ cups / 450 ml / 15 fl oz	Salt to taste	
Fish, sliced	20 gms	Oyster sauce	1 tsp / 5 ml
Prawns, sliced	20 gms	Egg, whisked	½
Mushroom, sliced	5 gms	Cornflour	1 tsp / 5 gms
Carrot, sliced	5 gms	Chinese wine	1 tsp / 5 ml
Crabmeat	10 gms	Green coriander, chopped	1 tsp / 5 gms

METHOD

- Heat chicken stock (1 cup) in a pan and blanch the fish, prawns, mushrooms and carrots in it. Remove and keep aside.
- Heat chicken stock (1¼ cups) in another pan, add the blanched fish, prawns, mushrooms and carrots along with crabmeat, salt to taste and oyster sauce. Cook for a few minutes.
- Add the egg through a strainer and thicken with cornflour dissolved in water.
- Stir in Chinese wine and remove from heat. Serve hot, garnished with chopped green coriander.

Hot and Sour Sharkfin with Chicken Soup

Serves - 4

Preparation time: 30 minutes

Cooking time: 10 minutes

INGREDIENTS

Sharkfins	40 gms / 1¼ oz
Ginger, chopped	2 tsp / 10 gms
Chinese wine	2 tsp / 10 ml
Vermicelli	10 gms
Black fungus	10 gms
Chicken stock	2 cups / 400 ml / 14 fl oz
Bamboo shoots	10 gms
Beancurd	10 gms
Chicken, boiled, shredded	10 gms
White pepper powder	2 tsp / 10 gms
Salt	2 tsp / 10 gms
Ajinomoto	1 tsp / 5 gms
Soya sauce	2 tsp / 10 ml
Black vinegar	2 tsp / 10 ml
Cornflour	1 tsp / 5 gms
Eggs, whisked	2
Chilli oil	1 tsp / 5 ml

METHOD

- Steam the sharkfins along with ginger and Chinese wine. Remove from heat and keep aside.
- Soak the vermicelli and the black fungus separately in water.
- Heat chicken stock in a pan, add the sharkfins along with vermicelli, black fungus, bamboo shoots, beancurd and chicken. Cook for a few minutes.
- Stir in the white pepper powder, salt, ajinomoto, soya sauce and black vinegar.
- Mix in cornflour dissolved in water to thicken the soup. Stir in the whisked egg and chilli oil.
- Remove from heat, transfer to a serving bowl and serve.

Sharkfin Crabmeat Soup

Serves - 4

Preparation time: 2 hours 30 minutes

Cooking time: 7 minutes

INGREDIENTS

Sharkfins, dry	60 gms / 2 oz	Salt to taste	
Chicken stock	12 cups / 2.4 lt	Ajinomoto	½ tsp / 3 gms
Ginger	60 gms / 2 oz	Oyster sauce	2 tsp / 10 ml
Chinese wine	3 tsp / 15 ml	Cornflour	1 tsp / 5 gms
Crab meat	60 gms / 2 oz	Egg, whisked	1

METHOD

- To improve the sharkfins, steam it along with chicken stock (10 cups), ginger and Chinese wine (2 tsp) for at least 3 hours. Remove from heat and keep aside.
- Heat 2 cups stock in a pan, add the sharkfins and crabmeat.
- Stir in the salt, ajinomoto and oyster sauce. Boil for a few minutes.
- Stir in cornflour dissolved in water to thicken the soup. Add egg and Chinese wine (1 tsp), stir and remove from heat.
- Transfer to serving bowls and serve hot.

Wonton Soup

Serves - 4

Preparation time: 15 minutes

Cooking time: 10 minutes

INGREDIENTS

Wonton skin	12	Chicken stock	4 cups / 800 ml / 28 fl oz
Chicken mince	60 gms / 2 oz	Spinach, chopped	10 gms
Salt to taste		Egg, whisked	1
Ajinomoto	1½ tsp / 8 gms	Chinese wine	1 tsp / 5 ml
Egg	1		

METHOD

- Mix the chicken mince along with salt, ajinomoto (½ tsp) and egg. Divide into 6 equal portions.
- Place one portion of the chicken mince mixture in the centre of the wonton skin and fold to close. Repeat the same process with the rest of the portions and the wonton skins.
- Blanch the prepared wontons and the spinach for a few minutes. Remove and keep aside.
- Heat the chicken stock in a pan, stir in the salt, ajinomoto (1 tsp), spinach and wontons.
- Cook for a few minutes, stir in the whisked egg and Chinese wine for flavour.
- Remove from heat, transfer to a serving bowl and serve hot.

Steamed Prawns with Ginger

Serves - 4

Preparation time: 20 minutes

Cooking time: 10 minutes

INGREDIENTS

Prawns, shelled	500 gms / 1.1 lb
Salt	1 tsp / 5 gms
Ajinomoto	1½ tsp / 8 gms
Eggs, whisked	2
Ginger, julienned	4 tsp / 20 gms
Chinese wine	2 tsp / 10 ml
Green coriander, chopped	2 tsp / 10 gms

METHOD

- Arrange the prawns neatly in a pan, add salt, ajinomoto, egg and ginger. Mix well.
- Cover the pan and steam the prawns for 10 minutes.
- Remove from heat, transfer to a serving bowl and pour Chinese wine on top.
- Serve immediately, garnished with green coriander.

Sesame Prawn Toast

Serves - 4

Preparation time: 15 minutes

Cooking time: 15 minutes

INGREDIENTS

Prawns, cleaned	500 gms / 1.1 lb	Ajinomoto	1 tsp / 5 gms
Ginger	2 tsp / 10 gms	Egg, whisked	2
Salt	1 tsp / 5 gms	Bread slices	8
Sesame oil	1 tsp / 5 ml	Sesame seeds, broiled	1 tbs / 15 gms
Chinese wine	1 tsp / 5 ml	Oil for frying	

METHOD

- Blend the prawns alongwith ginger, add salt, sesame oil, Chinese wine, ajinomoto and egg. Mix well.
- Divide the mixture into four equal portions and spread each portion over the bread slices evenly.
- Sprinkle sesame seeds on top and keep aside.
- Heat oil in a wok and deep fry the slices one by one till crisp on both sides.
- Drain excess oil and serve immediately, accompanied by sweet and sour sauce.

Vegetable Spring Rolls

Serves - 4

Preparation time: 30 minutes

Cooking time: 7 minutes

INGREDIENTS

Popia skin, large	12	Oil	5 tbs / 75 ml / 2½ fl oz
Carrot, julienned	40 gms / 1¼ oz	Garlic, chopped	2 tsp / 10 gms
Onions, julienned	40 gms / 1¼ oz	Salt to taste	
Cabbage, julienned	40 gms / 1¼ oz	Pepper	1½ tsp / 7 gms
Beansprout	20 gms	Ajinomoto	1 tsp / 5 gms

METHOD

- Heat oil in a deep pan and sauté garlic. Add all the vegetables, stir-fry for a few minutes.
- Stir in the salt, pepper and ajinomoto. Mix well and remove from heat.
- Spread the prepared vegetables over the spring roll skins and roll.
- Heat oil in a wok and deep fry the rolls till crisp and golden brown on all side. Remove, drain excess oil.
- Serve immediately, accompained by warm sweet and sour sauce.

Stir-Fried Mixed Vegetables

Serves - 4

Preparation time: 30 minutes

Cooking time: 10 minutes

INGREDIENTS

Button mushrooms, diced	40 gms / 1¼ oz	Vegetable stock	3 tbs / 45 ml / 1½ fl oz
Capcicum, diced	60 gms / 2 oz	Salt to taste	
Carrot, diced	40 gms / 1¼ oz	Ajinomoto	1 tsp / 5 gms
Cauliflower, diced	80 gms / 2¾ oz	Soya sauce	2 tsp / 10 ml
Cabbage, diced	80 gms / 2¾ oz	Cornflour	2 tsp / 10 gms
Sesame oil	4 tsp / 20 ml	Chinese wine	1½ tsp / 8 ml
Garlic, chopped	2 tsp / 10 gms	Almonds, slivered	20 gms

METHOD

- Blanch all the diced vegetables and keep aside.
- Heat sesame oil in a wok and sauté garlic for a few seconds. Add all the vegetables and toss for a few minutes.
- Stir in the vegetable stock, salt, ajinomoto, soya sauce and mix well.
- Add cornflour diluted in a little water to thicken and finish with Chinese wine and sesame oil.
- Remove from heat, transfer to a serving platter and serve immediately garnished with slivered almonds.

Stir-Fried Beansprouts

Serves - 4

Preparation time: 15 minutes

Cooking time: 5 minutes

INGREDIENTS

Beansprouts, cleaned	600 gms / 22 oz
Oil	2 tbs / 30 ml / 1 fl oz
Ginger, julienned	4 tsp / 20 gms
Carrot, julienned	60 gms / 2 oz
Spring onion, chopped	50 gms / 1¾ oz
Salt to taste	

METHOD

- Blanch the beansprouts and keep aside.
- Heat oil in a wok and sauté ginger.
- Add carrot and chopped spring onion. Stir-fry for a few minutes.
- Stir in the salt and mix well.
- Remove from heat onto a serving bowl and serve immediately.

Broccoli and Bamboo Shoot in Oyster Sauce

Serves - 4

Preparation time: 20 hours

Cooking time: 15 minutes

INGREDIENTS

Broccoli	230 gms / 8 oz
Salt to taste	
Oil	2 tsp / 10 ml
Garlic, chopped	1 tsp / 5 gms
Chicken stock	4 tbs / 60 ml / 2 fl oz
Soya sauce	1 tsp / 5 ml
Oyster sauce	4 tsp / 20 ml
Cornflour	½ tsp / 3 gms
Bamboo Shoot, sliced	30 gms / 1 oz
Chinese wine	½ tsp / 3 ml
Sesame oil	½ tsp / 3 ml

METHOD

- Cut the broccoli into small florets and blanch in salt water.
- Heat oil in a wok and sauté garlic till light brown. Stir in the chicken stock, soya sauce, salt and oyster sauce. Cook for a few minutes and add cornflour dissolved in water to thicken.
- Add bamboo shoots and cook further for 10 minutes. Finish with Chinese wine and sesame oil.
- Arrange the broccoli neatly on a serving platter and pour the prepared sauce on top. Serve hot.

Spinach, Black Mushroom and Babycorn

Serves - 4

Preparation time: 30 minutes

Cooking time: 10 minutes

INGREDIENTS

Spinach	300 gms / 11 oz
Babycorn	15 gms
Salt to taste	
Black mushrooms, dry	15 gms
Ginger	2 tsp / 10 gms
Oil	2 tsp / 10 ml
Garlic, chopped	1 tsp / 5 gms
Vegetable stock	3 tbs / 45 ml / 1½ fl oz
Soya sauce	2 tsp / 10 ml
Cornflour	1 tsp / 5 gms
Chinese wine	½ tsp / 3 ml
Sesame oil	½ tsp / 3 ml

METHOD

- Blanch the spinach and babycorn separately in salt water. Soak the black mushrooms overnight and steam with ginger.
- Heat oil in a pan and sauté garlic. Add vegetable stock alongwith soya sauce, salt to taste, babycorn and black mushrooms.
- Stir in cornflour dissolved in little water to thicken and finish with Chinese wine and sesame oil.
- Arrange the blanched spinach neatly on a serving platter and pour the prepared gravy on top. Serve hot.

Fried Chicken with Lemon Sauce

Serves - 4

Preparation time: 30 minutes

Cooking time: 15 minutes

INGREDIENTS

Chicken, leg	250 gms / 9 oz	Lemon juice	4 tsp / 20 ml
Salt to taste		Sugar	4 tsp / 20 gms
Ajinomoto	1 tsp / 5 gms	Water	2 tbs / 30 ml / 1 fl oz
Egg, whisked	1	Custard powder	2 tsp / 10 gms
Cornflour	5 tsp / 25 gms	Seasame seeds	1 tsp / 5 gms
Oil for deep fry			

METHOD

- Debone the chicken leg and flatten. Marinate with salt, ajinomoto, egg, cornflour (2 tsp) and custard powder.
- Heat oil in a pan and deep fry the chicken pieces till crisp on all sides. Remove from heat, cut into dices and keep aside.
- Prepare the lemon sauce, by mixing together lemon juice, sugar and water.
- Heat the prepared lemon sauce in a wok and stir in the cornflour (3 tsp) mixed with a little water and custard powder.
- Arrange the fried chicken pieces neatly on a serving platter and pour the prepared sauce.
- Garnish with sesame seeds and serve.

Crisp Fried Duck

Serves - 2-4

Preparation time: 6 hours

Cooking time: 15 minutes

INGREDIENTS

Duck, cleaned	1
Salt	2 tsp / 10 gms
Ajinomoto	2 tsp / 10 gms
Cloves	5
Cinnamon, whole	5
Ginger, chopped	15 gms
Spring onions, chopped	15 gms
Star anise	1 tsp / 5 gms
Oil	½ cup / 100 ml / 3½ fl oz
Plum sauce	2 tsp / 10 ml

METHOD

- Cut the duck into two halves and marinate with salt and ajinomoto. Keep aside for 3 hours.
- Steam the marinated duck with cloves, cinnamon, ginger, spring onions and star anise for 3 hours. Remove from heat and allow to cool. Drain the water completely.
- Heat oil in a wok and deep fry the steamed duck till it is crisp and golden brown.
- Remove, drain excess oil and serve hot, accompanied by plum sauce.

Chicken Finger Green Chilli

Serves - 4

Preparation time: 30 minutes

Cooking time: 10 minutes

INGREDIENTS

Chicken, julienned	250 gms / 9 oz
Salt to taste	
Egg, whisked	½
Cornflour	2 tsp / 10 gms
Oil	1 tsp / 5 ml + for frying
Ajinomoto	1 tsp / 5 gms
Ginger, chopped	1 tsp / 5 gms
Garlic, chopped	1 tsp / 5 gms
Spring onions, chopped	5 gms
Green chillies, chopped	2 tsp / 10 gms
Five spice powder	½ tsp / 3 gms
Black peppercorns, crushed	1 tsp / 5 gms
Chinese wine	1 tsp / 5 ml

METHOD

- Marinate the chicken with salt, egg, cornflour, oil and ajinomoto. Keep aside.
- Heat oil in a pan and deep fry the marinated chicken pieces. Remove and keep aside.
- Add ginger, garlic, spring onions and green chillies in the same pan and sauté for a few minutes.
- Add the fried chicken along with five spice powder, black peppercorns and toss well.
- Stir in Chinese wine and remove from heat. Serve hot.

Note: Five spice powder consists of five spices mixed together: clove powder, cinnamon powder, star anise powder, Szechurian black pepper and fennel powder.

Chicken Cashew Nut Green Pepper

Serves - 2-4

Preparation time: 40 minutes

Cooking time: 10 minutes

INGREDIENTS

Chicken, diced	500 gms / 1.1 lb	Cashew Nuts,	60 gms / 2 oz
Salt to taste		Garlic, chopped	20 gms
Ajinomoto	1 tsp / 5 gms	Capsicum, diced	40 gms / 1¼ fl oz
Egg, whisked	1	Chicken stock	3 tbs / 45 ml / 1½ fl oz tbs
Cornflour	4 tsp / 20 gms	Soya sauce	4 tsp / 20 ml
Oil	4½ tbs / 70 ml / 2¼ fl oz	Chinese wine	4 tsp / 20 ml
	+for marination	Sesame oil	2 tsp / 10 ml

METHOD

- Marinate the chicken pieces with salt, ajinomoto, egg, cornflour and oil.
- Heat oil (4 tbs) in a pan, stir-fry the marinated chicken pieces. Remove and keep aside.
- In the same pan, deep fry the cashew nuts and keep aside.
- In a wok, heat oil (½ tsp) sauté chopped garlic and add capsicum, cashew nuts, stock, soya sauce, salt and ajinomoto. Mix well and cook for a few minutes.
- Stir in the cornflour dissolved in water to thicken and finish with Chinese wine and sesame oil.
- Remove from heat onto a serving bowl and serve.

Chicken with Dry Chilli Sauce

Serves - 4

Preparation time: 30 minutes

Cooking time: 10 minutes

INGREDIENTS

Chicken boneless, cut into dices	560 gms / 20 oz
Salt to taste	
Ajinomoto	1 tsp / 5 gms
Egg, whisked	1
Cornflour	4 tsp / 20 gms
Oil	4 tbs / 60 ml / 2 fl oz + for frying
Red chillies whole, quartered	30 gms / 1 oz
Garlic	2 tsp / 10 gms
Spring onions, diced	60 gms / 2 oz
Ginger, julienned	2 tsp / 10 gms
Dry chilli sauce	4 tbs / 60 ml / 2 fl oz

METHOD

- Marinate the chicken pieces with salt, ajinomoto, egg, cornflour and oil.
- Heat oil in a pan, add the marinated chicken pieces and stir-fry for a few minutes. Remove, drain excess oil and keep aside.
- In the same pan, add the red chillies along with garlic and sauté till they turn dark brown in colour.
- Add the chicken pieces, spring onion whites and ginger. Mix well and stir in the dry chilli sauce.
- Add cornflour dissolved in water to thicken the sauce. Stir and remove from heat.
- Garnish with spring onions and serve.

Pork Coins with Honey

Serves - 2-4

Preparation time: 20 minutes + 2 hours for marination

Cooking time: 10 minutes

INGREDIENTS

Pork, cut into pieces	500 gms / 1.1 lb	Onions, diced	60 gms / 2 oz
Eggs, whisked	2	Tomato, diced	60 gms / 2 oz
Custard powder	2 tsp / 10 gms	Pineapple, diced	60 gms / 2 oz
Cornflour	2 tsp / 10 gms	Honey sauce	½ cup / 120 ml / 4 fl oz
Salt	1 tsp / 5 gms		

METHOD

- Marinate the pork pieces with egg, custard powder, cornflour and salt. Keep aside for 2 hours.
- Skewer the pork pieces alternatively along with diced onions, tomato and pineapple.
- Cook on a charcoal grill till completely done.
- Coat the skewers with honey sauce and cook further for a few seconds.
- Remove the skewers from the grill and allow excess liquid to drip.
- Serve hot.

Braised Sea Cucumber with Crabmeat

Serves - 4

Preparation time: 4 hours

Cooking time: 15 minutes

INGREDIENTS

Sea cucumber	200 gms / 7 oz	Oyster sauce	1 tsp / 5 ml
Crabmeat	40 gms / 1¼ oz	Soya sauce	1 tsp / 5 ml
Carrot, diced	10 gms	Salt	1 tsp / 5 gms
Mushrooms, diced	10 gms	Ajinomoto	1 tsp / 5 gms
Oil	2 tsp / 10 ml	Cornflour	2 tsp / 10 gms
Garlic, chopped	3 gms	Spring onions, chopped	10 gms
Chicken stock	1 tsp / 5 ml	Chinese wine	½ tsp / 3 ml

METHOD

- Soak the sea cucumber in hot water for at least 8-10 days so that it regains its original shape or cut the sea cucumber into dices and boil in water on low heat for 4 hours.
- Blanch the carrot and mushroom and keep aside.
- Heat oil in a wok, sauté garlic, add the mushrooms, carrots and the sea cucumber. Mix well.
- Stir in the chicken stock, oyster sauce, soya sauce, salt, ajinomoto, and crabmeat. Mix and cook for a few minutes.
- Stir in the cornflour dissolved in water to thicken the sauce.
- Add spring onions and Chinese wine. Stir and remove from heat.
- Transfer to a serving bowl and serve.

Sweet and Sour Fish

Serves - 4

Preparation time: 40 minutes

Cooking time: 10 minutes

INGREDIENTS

Fish, fillets, diced	500 gms / 1.1 lb
Eggs, whisked	2
Salt	2 tsp / 10 gms
Custard powder	2 tsp / 10 gms
Cornflour	6 tsp / 30 gms / 1 oz
Oil	4 tsp / 20 ml + for frying
Capsicum, chopped	40 gms / 1¼ oz
Onions, chopped	40 gms / 1¼ oz
Sweet and sour sauce	½ cup / 120 ml / 4 fl oz
Pineapple, diced	40 gms / 1¼ oz
Tomato, chopped	40 gms / 1¼ oz

METHOD

- Marinate the fish fillets with egg, salt, custard powder and cornflour (2 tsp).
- Heat oil in a pan, and deep fry the marinated fish fillet.
- Remove, drain excess oil and keep aside.
- In the same pan sauté capsicum and onions. Stir in the sweet and sour sauce along with pineapple and tomato. Cook for a few minutes.
- Dissolve cornflour (4 tsp) in water and add to thicken the sauce. Stir and remove from heat.
- Transfer the fried fish pieces onto a serving platter. Pour the prepared sauce on top and serve.

Stir-Fried Abalone with Black Mushroom

Serves - 4

Preparation time: 20 minutes

Cooking time: 20 minutes

INGREDIENTS

Abalone	300 gms / 11 oz
Spinach	300 gms / 11 oz
Oil	2 tsp / 10 ml
Garlic, chopped	15 gms
Chicken stock	1 cup / 200 ml / 7 fl oz
Soya sauce	4 tsp / 20 ml
Oyster sauce	2 tsp / 10 ml
Salt to taste	
Black mushrooms	200 gms / 7 oz
Cornflour	2 tsp / 10 gms
Sesame oil	2 tsp / 10 ml
Chinese wine	2 tsp / 10 ml

METHOD

- Wash the abalone and slice thickly. Boil the spinach and keep aside.
- Heat oil in a wok, add garlic and sauté. Stir in the chicken stock, soya sauce, oyster sauce and salt to taste. Mix well and cook for 5 minutes.
- Add the sliced abalone along with black mushrooms. Stir in cornflour dissolved in little water to thicken.
- Cook until the abalone is tender. Stir in sesame oil and Chinese wine and remove from heat.
- Spread the boiled spinach on a serving platter and pour the cooked abalone over it. Serve hot.

Prawns in Garlic Sauce

Serves - 4

Preparation time: 25 minutes

Cooking time: 10 minutes

INGREDIENTS

Prawns, cleaned	600 gms / 22 oz
Onion, chopped	10 gms
Oil	8 tsp / 40 ml
Salt	2 tsp / 10 gms
Pepper to taste	
Ajinomoto	1 tsp / 5 gms
Egg, whisked	1
Cornflour	3 tsp / 15 gms
Chicken stock	4 tsp / 20 ml

For the Garlic Sauce:

Ginger, minced	100 gms / 3½ oz
Garlic, minced	200 gms / 7 oz
Red Chilli paste (pg. ii)	40 gms/ 1¼ oz
Tomato ketchup	2 cups / 400 gm
Salt	1 tsp / 5 gms
Sugar	4 tbs / 60 gms / 2 oz
Ajinomoto	1 tsp / 5 gms
Rice vinegar	8 tsp / 40 ml / 1¼ fl oz
Sesame oil	2 tbs / 30 ml / 1 fl oz

METHOD

- Marinate the prawns with salt, pepper, ajinomoto, egg and cornflour. Keep aside.
- For the garlic sauce, blend together ginger, garlic and chillies along with tomato ketchup. Stir in the seasoning, sugar, ajinomoto, rice vinegar, and sesame oil.
- Heat oil in a pan and stir-fry the marinated prawns for a few minutes. Remove and keep aside.
- In the same pan, sauté onion, stir in the garlic sauce alongwith chicken stock, prawns and ajinomoto. Mix well and cook for a few minutes.
- Stir in the cornflour mixed with water to thicken.
- Remove from heat, transfer to a serving bowl and serve.

Lobster in Black Bean Sauce

Serves - 4

Preparation time: 30 minutes

Cooking time: 15 minutes

INGREDIENTS

Lobster, cleaned	800 gms / 28 oz
Salt to taste	
Ajinomoto	1 tsp / 5 gms
Egg, whisked	1
Cornflour	2 tbs / 30 gms / 1 oz
Oil	¾ cup / 150 ml / 5 fl oz
Garlic, chopped	20 gms
Capsicum, chopped	40 gms /1¼ oz
Onions, chopped	40 gms / 1¼ oz
Mushrooms, chopped	40 gms / 1¼ oz
Black beans	40 gms / 1¼ oz
Red chilli paste (pg. ii)	2 tsp / 10 gms
Chicken stock	8 tsp / 40 ml / 1¼ fl oz
Soya sauce	4 tsp / 20 ml
Seasame oil	2 tsp / 10 ml
Chinese wine	1 tsp / 5 ml

METHOD

- Remove the lobster meat from the shell and cut into pieces. Keep the shell aside.
- Marinate the pieces, with salt, ajinomoto, egg and cornflour.
- Heat oil (½ cup) in a wok and fry the empty lobster shell. Remove and keep aside.
- In the same wok fry the marinated lobster meat pieces, remove, drain excess oil and keep aside.
- In a separate wok heat oil (¼ cup) and sauté garlic. Add the chopped vegetables along with black beans, chilli paste, chicken stock, soya sauce, salt to taste, ajinomoto and the fried meat pieces. Mix well and cook for two minutes on medium heat.
- Stir in the cornflour dissolved in water to thicken the sauce. Finish with seasame oil and Chinese wine.
- Remove from heat. Carefully transfer the prepared dish in the lobster shell and serve.

Vegetable Fried Noodles

Serves - 4

Preparation time: 15 minutes

Cooking time: 5 minutes

INGREDIENTS

Noodles	600 gms / 28 oz
Oil	5 tbs / 75 ml / 2½ fl oz
Garlic, chopped	40 gms / 1¼ oz
Cabbage, shredded	120 gms / 4 oz
Carrot, shredded	40 gm / 1¼ fl oz
Onions	90 gms / 3 oz
Beansprouts	40 gms /1¼ oz
Capsicum, shredded	40 gms /1¼ oz
Salt to taste	
Vegetable stock	4 tsp / 20 ml
Soya sauce	3 tsp / 15 ml
Lea and Perrins sauce	3 tsp / 15 ml
Ajinomoto	2 tsp / 10 gms

METHOD

- Boil the noodles and spread on a clean table top to cool. Sprinkle oil (2½ tbs) on the noodles.
- Heat oil (2½ tbs) in a wok and sauté garlic. Add the vegetables and mix well.
- Stir in the vegetable stock, seasoning, soya sauce, Lea and Perrins sauce, ajinomoto and noodles. Mix well and stir-fry till the moisture evaporates and the vegetables are crunchy.
- Remove from heat, transfer to a serving platter and serve.

Crispy Noodles with Sweet and Sour Sauce

Serves - 4

Preparation time: 30 minutes

Cooking time: 15 minutes

INGREDIENTS

Noodles, boiled	180 gms / 6 oz	Tomato, diced	20 gms
Oil for frying		Capsicum, diced	20 gms
Tomato ketchup	4 tbs / 60 ml / 2 fl oz	Onion, diced	10 gms
Lea & Perrins sauce	1 tsp / 5 ml	Pineapple, diced	10 gms
Apricot jam	1 tsp / 5 gms	Cabbage, diced	10 gms
Sugar	2 tsp / 10 gms	Cornflour	1 tsp / 5 gms
Vinegar	½ tsp / 3 ml		

METHOD

- Heat oil in a wok, add the boiled noodles and deep fry till crisp and golden brown. Drain excess oil and keep aside.
- Prepare the sweet and sour sauce by mixing together tomato ketchup, Lea and Perrins sauce, apircot jam, sugar and a little water. Heat this mixture in a pan till it comes to a boil.
- Remove from heat and add vinegar. Mix well and allow to cool.
- Heat oil in a pan and sauté tomato and pineapple along with all the vegetables. Add the prepared sweet and sour sauce and mix well. Stir in cornflour dissolved in water to thicken and remove from heat.
- Arrange the fried noodles neatly on a serving platter. Pour the sweet and sour sauce on top and serve.

Rice Vermicelli with Vegetables

Serves - 4

Preparation time: 1 hour

Cooking time: 5 minutes

INGREDIENTS

Rice vermicelli	200 gms / 7 oz	Lea and Perrins sauce	1 tsp / 5 ml
Oil	1 tbs / 15 ml	Soya sauce	1 tsp / 5 ml
Garlic	1 tsp / 5 gms	Carrot, julienned	25 gms
Vegetable stock	5 tsp / 25 ml	Cabbage, julienned	25 gms
Salt	1 tsp / 5 gms	Beansprouts	25 gms
Ajinomoto	½ tsp / 3 gms	Spring onions, chopped	25 gms

METHOD

- Soak the vermicelli for at least one hour in cold water.
- Heat oil in a wok and sauté garlic, stir in the vegetable stock, salt, ajinomoto, Lea and Perrins sauce and soya sauce.
- Add all the vegetables and the rice vermicelli.
- Mix well and cook for a few minutes till the liquids dry up and the vegetables are cooked but still crunchy.
- Remove from heat onto a serving platter and serve.

Babycorn, Capsicum and Mushroom Fried Rice

Serves - 4

Preparation time: 20 minutes

Cooking time: 10 minutes

INGREDIENTS

Rice, boiled	560 gms / 20 oz
Oil	1 tbs / 15 ml
Mushrooms, boiled, diced	40 gms / 1¼ oz
Babycorn, boiled, diced	40 gms / 1¼ oz
Capsicum, diced	40 gms / 1¼ oz
Salt to taste	
Ajinomoto	1½ tsp / 8 gms

METHOD

- Heat oil in a pan and sauté mushrooms, babycorn and capsicum for a few minutes.
- Add the boiled rice to the pan along with salt and ajinomoto.
- Stir-fry for a few minutes and remove from heat and serve hot.

Vegetable Fried Rice

Serves - 4

Preparation time: 45 minutes

Cooking time: 7 minutes

INGREDIENTS

Rice, boiled	600 gms / 22 oz
Oil	2 tbs / 30 ml / 1 fl oz
Mushrooms, boiled, chopped	40 gms / 1¼ oz
Carrots, boiled, chopped	40 gms / 1¼ oz
Green peas, boiled	40 gms / 1¼ oz
Salt	4 tsp / 20 gms
Sesame oil	2 tsp / 10 ml
Spring onions, chopped	20 gms

METHOD

- Heat oil in a wok, add mushrooms, carrots and green peas. Stir-fry for a few minutes.
- Add the boiled rice, salt and mix well.
- Stir in the sesame oil for flavour.
- Remove from heat onto a serving bowl and serve hot, garnished with spring onions.

Yang Chow Fried Rice

Serves - 4

Preparation time: 30 minutes

Cooking time: 5 minutes

INGREDIENTS

Boiled rice, cooled	400 gms / 14 oz	Spring onions, chopped	20 gms
Pork, roasted, diced	40 gms / 1¼ oz	Oil	8 tsp / 40 ml / 1¼ fl oz
Shrimps, boiled	40 gms / 1¼ oz	Egg, whisked	1
Peas	20 gms	Salt to taste	

METHOD

- Heat the rice slightly to seperate out the grains. Heat oil (4 tsp) in a pan, add the egg and fry, remove and keep aside.
- Heat the remaining oil in the same pan, add the diced pork and boiled shrimps. Sauté for a few minutes.
- Add rice along with peas and spring onions. Toss well and stir in the salt to taste.
- Remove from heat, garnish with fried egg and serve hot.

Ice Cream Pancake with Honey and Walnuts

Serves - 4

Preparation time: 30 minutes

Cooking time: 10 minutes

INGREDIENTS

Flour	1 cup / 200 gms / 7 oz	Egg	1
Sugar	$5^1/_3$ tbs / 80 gms / 2¾ oz	Water as required	
Honey	4 tsp / 20 ml	Oil	4 tsp / 20 ml
Walnuts	120 gms / 4 oz	Vanilla ice cream	10-15 scoops

METHOD

- Chop the walnuts into halves. Heat sugar to caramalize slightly and add honey.
- In a mixing bowl, mix flour along with egg and oil. Add water and mix to a smooth batter.
- Make small pancakes and keep aside. Roll the pancakes with vanilla ice cream and cut the pancake into two.
- Serve immediately, garnished with chocolate sauce, caramalized honey and walnuts.

Candied Apple

Serves - 4

Preparation time: 30 minutes

Cooking time: 10 minutes

INGREDIENTS

Apple	2
Flour	1 cup / 200 gms / 7 oz
Eggs	2
Cornflour	4 tsp / 20 gms
Custard powder (vanilla)	2 tsp / 10 gms
Water as required	
Oil	30 ml / 2 tbs + for frying
Castor sugar	120 gms / 4 oz
Water	3 tbs / 40 ml / 1¼ fl oz

METHOD

- Peel and remove the seeds from the apple, cut into slices.
- Make a thick batter by mixing together flour, eggs, cornflour, custard powder and water.
- Heat oil in a wok, dip the apple slices in the batter and deep fry. Remove, drain excess oil.
- In a separate wok, heat sugar along with a little oil and water till it reaches a thread-like consistency.
- Dip the apple slices in the sugar syrup to coat evenly.
- Remove carefully from the sugar syrup and dip in ice water for a few minutes. Serve immediately.

Szechuan Pancake

Serves - 4

Preparation time: 30 minutes

Cooking time: 10 minutes

INGREDIENTS

Dates	160 gms / 5 oz
Oil	4 tbs / 60 ml / 2 fl oz + for frying
Eggs, whisked	2
Flour	½ cup / 120 gms / 4 oz
Cornflour	5 tsp / 25 gms
Custard powder	2 tsp / 10 gms
Water as required	

METHOD

- For the date paste, mince the dates after removing the seeds. Heat oil (4 tbs) in a pan and fry the minced dates. Remove from heat and allow to cool.
- Prepare a batter by mixing together eggs, flour, cornflour, custard powder and water. Keep aside for 30 minutes.
- Divide the batter in equal portions and roll out into pancakes with a rolling pin.
- Make small balls of the date paste and flatten evenly on the pancakes.
- Fold the pancake to form a rectangle and seal the edges.
- Heat oil in a pan and deep fry the pancakes till golden brown in colour. Drain excess oil and serve.

Toffee Banana

Serves - 4

Preparation time: 20 minutes

Cooking time: 10 minutes

INGREDIENTS

Bananas, cut into big pieces	4	Water as required	
Eggs, whisked	2	Oil	4 tsp / 20 ml + for frying
Flour	2 tsp / 10 gms	Castor sugar	2½ cups / 500 gms / 1.1 lb
Cornflour	1 tsp / 5 gms	Sesame seeds	1 tbs / 15 gms
Custard powder (vanilla)	2 tsp / 10 gms		

METHOD

- Prepare a batter by mixing together eggs, flour, cornflour, custard powder and water.
- Heat oil in a wok, dip the banana pieces in the batter and deep fry. Remove, drain excess oil and keep aside.
- In a separate wok, cook the castor sugar alongwith water and oil till it turns golden in colour.
- Dip the fried banana pieces in the sugar syrup to coat evenly. Remove, drain excess syrup and keep aside.
- Sprinkle sesame seeds on top and dip in ice water for a few minutes. Remove and serve.

Thai

For a place which cultivates the rice crop widely and is watered by myriad waterways, developing a highly sophisticated cuisine based primarily on rice and fish has been a logical progression in Thailand. Trade with the East Indies brought cloves and nutmeg to ancient Thailand, while South America gave it the pungent chilli pepper. Soon Thai food came to be identified with seasonings both hot and subtle. The Thai *kapi*, shrimp paste made with condiments like salt, pepper, ginger, cinnamon, cloves, garlic, white onions, nutmeg and several strongly flavoured herbs, give Thai food its unique character. Rice noodles, meat or fish curries in coconut milk, crisp salads (*yam*), soups (*tom yum*), a spicy hot dipping sauce (*nam prig*) comprise a typical Thai meal.

Por Pia Savoey

Serves - 4

Thai Spring Rolls

Preparation time: 25 minutes

Cooking time: 10 minutes

INGREDIENTS

Vermicelli	½ cup / 120 gms / 4 oz
Water as required	
Cabbage	120 gms / 4 oz
Carrots	60 gms / 2 oz
Spring onions	40 gms / 1¼ oz
Onions	60 gms / 2 oz
Oil	4 tbs / 60 ml / 2 fl oz + for frying
Salt to taste	
Pepper to taste	
Soya sauce	2 tsp / 10 ml
Spring roll skins	16
Plum sauce	½ cup / 100 ml / 3½ fl oz

METHOD

- Soak vermicelli in water for 10 minutes.
- Shred the cabbage, carrots, spring onions and onions. Keep aside.
- Heat oil (1 tbs) in a pan, add the chopped vegetables and sauté for a few minutes.
- Add vermicelli, salt to taste, pepper to taste and soya sauce. Sauté further for a few seconds.
- Remove from heat and keep on a perforated vessel to cool. Divide the mixture into 4 equal portions.
- Roll the portions into the spring roll skins and deep fry in hot oil. Remove and keep aside.
- Serve hot, accompanied by plum sauce.

Satay Kai

Serves - 4

Chicken Satay Sticks

Preparation time: 20 minutes
+ 4 hours for marination
Cooking time: 10 minutes

INGREDIENTS

Chicken boneless	600 gms / 22 oz	Fish sauce	½ cup / 100 ml / 3½ fl oz
Curry powder	8 tsp / 40 gms / 1¼ oz	Lemon grass, chopped	40 gms / 1¼ oz
Garlic cloves	45 gms / 1½ oz	Galangal (Kha), chopped	25 gms
Coriander root	40 gms / 1¼ oz	Cumin seeds	4 tsp / 20 gms
Coriander seeds	1 tbs / 15 gms	Peanut sauce	½ cup / 100 ml / 3½ fl oz
White pepper powder	4 tsp / 20 gms		

METHOD

- Cut the chicken into 2 inch broad strips.
- Make a paste by mixing together curry powder, garlic cloves, coriander root and coriander seeds, white pepper powder, fish sauce, lemon grass, galangal and cumin seeds.
- Marinate the chicken strips in the prepared paste for 4-5 hours.
- Skewer the chicken strips on bamboo sticks and serve hot, accompanied by peanut sauce.

Thord Man Koong

Serves - 4

Ground Fish mixed with Thai spices, deep fried and served with sauce

Preparation time: 30 minutes
Cooking time: 15 minutes

INGREDIENTS

Prawns	400 gms / 14 oz
Pork fat	80 gms / 2¾ oz
Fish sauce	4 tbs / 60 ml / 2 fl oz
Chinese wine	4 tsp / 20 ml
White pepper powder	12 tsp / 0 gms
Cornflour	4 tsp / 20 gms
Sesame oil	4 tsp / 20 ml
Light soya sauce	4 tsp / 20 ml
Breadcrumbs	1 cup / 200 gms / 7 oz
Oil for frying	
Plum sauce	½ cup / 100 ml / 3½ fl oz

METHOD

- Shell and clean the prawns. Mince the prawns and pork fat together.
- To the prawn mixture, add fish sauce, Chinese wine, white pepper powder, cornflour, sesame oil, soya sauce and mix well.
- Shape into small round cutlets. Coat with breadcrumbs and deep fry in hot oil until golden brown in colour.
- Remove, drain excess oil and place neatly on a serving platter.
- Serve hot, accompanied by plum sauce.

Som Tum

Serves - 4

A tangy salad made from young papayas with a hint of chillies

Preparation time: 15 minutes

Cooking time: 5 minutes

INGREDIENTS

Raw papaya	1 kg / 2.2 lb	Red chillies, whole	6
Tomatoes, chopped	240 gms / 9 oz	Fish sauce to taste	
Peanuts	180 gms / 6 oz	Lemon juice	3 tbs / 45 ml / 1½ fl oz
Garlic cloves	6-8	Sugar	2 tbs / 30 gms / 1 oz

METHOD

- Shred the papaya and chop the tomatoes.
- Pound the peanuts, garlic cloves and red chillies in a mortar and pestle. Remove to a bowl.
- Add the shredded papaya to the peanut mixture along with chopped tomatoes, fish sauce, lemon juice and sugar. Mix well.
- Remove to a serving dish and serve immediately.

Tom Yam Koong

Serves - 4

A spicy hot broth with prawns

Preparation time: 15 minutes

Cooking time: 10 minutes

INGREDIENTS

Mushrooms	150 gms / 5 oz
Lemon grass	80 gms / 2¾ oz
Lemon leaves	6
Red chillies	4
Galangal (Kha)	80 gms / 2¾ oz
Prawn stock	4 cups / 800 ml
Prawns, cleaned	150 gms / 5 oz
Fish sauce	1 tbs / 30 ml / 1 fl oz
Chilli paste	1 tbs / 30 gms / 1 oz
Tamarind extract	3 tbs / 45 ml / 1½ fl oz
Lemon juice	4 tbs / 60 ml / 2 fl oz

METHOD

- Chop the lemon grass, lemon leaves and red chillies. Slice the mushrooms and galangal.
- Heat the prawn stock in a pan and add the chopped vegetables.
- Stir in the prawns, fish sauce, chilli paste, tamarind extract and lemon juice.
- Simmer and cook for 5-10 minutes or until the vegetables are tender. Remove from heat
- Transfer to a soup bowl and serve hot.

Kaeng Jued Woon Sen Koong

Serves - 4

Chicken soup with vermicelli, prawns and pork quennels

Preparation time: 15 minutes
Cooking time: 20 minutes

INGREDIENTS

Chicken stock	4 cups / 800 ml / 28 fl oz	Mushrooms, chopped	80 gms / 2¾ oz
Vermicelli	240 gms / 9 oz	Fish sauce to taste	
Celery	80 gms / 2¾ oz	White pepper powder	pinch or two
Spring onions	40 gms / 1¼ oz	Garlic, chopped	20 gms
Chicken, minced	240 gms / 9 oz	Green coriander	4-8 sprigs
Prawns, cleaned	80 gms / 2¾ oz		

METHOD

- Soak vermicelli in sufficient water. Drain and keep aside. Cut the celery and spring onions into pieces.
- Divide the chicken mince into equal portions and shape into balls.
- Heat the chicken stock in a wok, add the chicken balls and prawns. Bring to a boil.
- Add mushrooms, fish sauce and white pepper powder. Simmer for 15-20 minutes.
- In a soup bowl, place vermicelli along with celery, garlic and spring onions.
- Pour the prepared soup on top and serve hot, garnished with green coriander.

Tom Kha Kai

Serves - 4

Mildly spiced soup with chicken, lemon grass and galangal in coconut milk

Preparation time: 15 minutes
Cooking time: 10 minutes

INGREDIENTS

Chicken (boneless cubes)	360 gms / 12 oz
Mushrooms	120 gms / 4 oz
Lemon grass	50 gms / 1¾ oz
Red chillies	4
Coconut milk	3 cups / 600 ml / 22 fl oz
Galangal (Kha)	60 gms / 2 oz
Lemon leaves	6-8
Fish sauce	3 tbs / 45 ml / 1¼ fl oz
Lemon juice	4 tbs / 60 ml / 2 fl oz
Green coriander	4-6 sprigs
Chilli oil	1 tsp / 5 ml

METHOD

- Cut the chicken into dices. Slice the mushrooms and galangal. Cut the lemon grass and red chillies into pieces.
- Heat coconut milk in a pan, add mushrooms, galangal, lemon grass and red chillies.
- Stir in the fish sauce and lemon juice.
- Boil for 5-6 minutes and remove from heat.
- Serve hot, garnished with green coriander and chilli oil.

Tom Kha Kai (Veg)

Serves - 4

Mildly spiced soup with mushroom, lemon grass and galangal in coconut milk

Preparation time: 15 minutes
Cooking time: 10 minutes

INGREDIENTS

Mushrooms	120 gms / 4 oz	Lemon leaves	6
Lemon grass	80 gms / 2¾ oz	Fish sauce	1 tbs / 30 ml / 1 fl oz
Red chillies	4	Lemon juice	4 tbs / 60 ml / 2 fl oz
Coconut milk	2 cups / 400 ml / 14 fl oz	Green coriander	3-6 sprigs
Galangal (Kha)	80 gms / 2¾ oz	Chilli oil	1 tsp / 5 ml

METHOD

- Slice the mushrooms and kha. Cut the lemon grass and red chillies into pieces.
- Heat coconut milk in a pan, add mushrooms, galangal, lemon grass and red chillies.
- Stir in the fish sauce and lemon juice.
- Boil for 5-6 minutes and remove from heat.
- Serve hot, garnished with green coriander and chilli oil.

Panaeng Tao Hoo Kap Het

Serves - 4

Tofu and mushrooms stir-fried in sauce

Preparation time: 15 minutes

Cooking time: 15 minutes

INGREDIENTS

Tofu, diced	500 gms / 1.1 lb	Capsicum, diced	120 gms / 4 oz
Mushrooms, cut into halves	300 gms / 11 oz	Fish sauce / Salt to taste	
Panaeng curry paste	200 gms / 7 oz	Red chillies	4
Lemon leaves	6	Green chillies	4
Basil leaves	10-12	Coconut milk	2 cups / 400 ml / 14 fl oz
Onion, diced	120 gms / 4 oz	Oil for frying	

METHOD

- Heat oil in a pan and deep fry the diced tofu till golden brown. Remove and keep aside.
- Blanch the mushrooms and keep aside.
- In a pan, heat Panaeng curry paste, add the fried tofu, mushrooms, capsicum and onions. Sauté for a minute.
- Stir in coconut milk and bring to a boil. Add the remaining ingredients and cook on low heat for 10 minutes. (if required add vegetable stock).
- Serve hot, accompanied by steamed rice.

Phad Phak Ruam Mit

Serves - 4

An assortment of garden vegetables, stir-fried with soya sauce

Preparation time: 20 minutes

Cooking time: 10 minutes

INGREDIENTS

Carrots	200 gms / 7 oz
Cabbage	240 gms / 9 oz
Cauliflower	240 gms / 9 oz
Babycorn	240 gms / 9 oz
Mushrooms	240 gms / 9 oz
Garlic	40 gms / 1¼ oz
Soya sauce	2 tsp / 10 ml
Salt to taste	
Pepper to taste	
Sugar a pinch	
Oil	½ cup / 100 ml / 3½ fl oz

METHOD

- Cut the carrots in small quarters and the cabbage into big quarters. Remove small florets from the cauliflower and cut the mushrooms into halves. Blanch all the vegetables including babycorn.
- Heat oil in a wok, add garlic and sauté.
- Add the blanched vegetables and sauté further over high heat.
- Stir in soya sauce, salt to taste, pepper to taste and sugar. Mix well.
- Remove from heat and serve hot.

Phad Het Kap Met Mamaung

Serves - 4

Mushrooms stir-fried with green chilli and cashewnuts

Preparation time: 20 minutes

Cooking time: 10 minutes

INGREDIENTS

Mushrooms	600 gms / 22 oz
Cashew nuts	240 gms / 9 oz
Spring onions	120 gms / 4 oz
Onions	120 gms / 4 oz
Capsicum	80 gms / 2¾ oz
Red chillies, dry, roasted	4
Green chillies	2
Garlic, chopped	20 gms
Salt to taste	
Pepper to taste	
Oil	¾ cup / 150 ml / 4 fl oz

METHOD

- Cut mushrooms into quarters and blanch, fry cashewnuts till golden brown.
- Cut the onions and capsicum into discs, spring onions and green chillies into big pieces.
- Heat oil in a wok and sauté garlic. Add the remaining ingredients and toss on high heat. Add a little stock if required.
- Serve hot, accompanied by steamed rice.

Kai Yang

Serves - 4

Whole chicken marinated overnight in Thai herbs and cooked over a charcoal grill

Preparation time: 15 minutes
+ 4 hours for marination
Cooking time: 20 minutes

INGREDIENTS

Chicken	1.5 kg / 3.3 lb	Fish sauce	3 tbs / 45 ml / 1½ fl oz
Lemon grass	40 gms / 1¼ oz	White pepper powder	3 tsp / 15 gms
Galangal (Kha)	40 gms / 1¼ oz	Soya sauce	4 tsp / 20 ml
Coriander root	50 gms / 1¾ oz	Kao wine	4 tsp / 20 ml
Garlic	40 gms / 1¼ oz	Sweet chilli sauce	4 tbs / 60 gms / 2 oz

METHOD

- Chop lemon grass, galangal, coriander root and garlic.
- Mix the chopped vegetables along with fish sauce, white pepper powder, soya sauce, kao wine and sweet chilli sauce. Blend to make a smooth paste.
- Cut the backbone of the chicken into two and flatten.
- Marinate the chicken in the prepared paste and keep aside for 4-5 hours.
- Skewer the chicken and grill over a charcoal grill until cooked.
- Remove from skewers and serve hot, accompanied by steamed rice and Tom Yam Koong (page i).

Kai Yad Sai

Serves - 4

Chicken omelette

Preparation time: 25 minutes

Cooking time: 10 minutes

INGREDIENTS

Mushrooms	360 gms / 12 oz
Carrots	180 gms / 6 oz
Onions	180 gms / 6 oz
Capsicum	80 gms / 2¾ oz
Babycorn	80 gms / 2¾ oz
Green peas	180 gms / 6 oz
Chicken, minced	200 gms / 7 oz
Tomato ketchup	45 ml / 1½ fl oz
Fish sauce	2 tbs / 30 ml / 1 fl oz
Oyster sauce	1 tsp / 5 ml
Maggi sauce (optional)	1 tsp / 5 ml
Soya sauce	2 tsp / 10 ml
Pepper	1 tsp / 5 gms
Oil	¾ cup / 150 ml / 5 fl oz
Eggs, whisked	3

METHOD

- Chop the mushrooms, carrots, onions, capsicum and babycorn.
- Heat oil in a wok and sauté the chicken mince until light brown.
- Add the chopped vegetables along with green peas, tomato ketchup, fish sauce, oyster sauce, maggi sauce, soya sauce and pepper. Mix well and cook until vegetables are tender. Remove from heat and keep aside.
- Heat oil in a pan, add the beaten eggs to make a thin omlette. Remove and keep aside.
- Place the prepared mixture in the centre of the omlette and fold like a parcel.
- Remove to a dish and serve.

Kai Phad Khing

Serves - 4

Stir-fried chicken with ginger, spring onions and pineapple

Preparation time: 20 minutes
Cooking time: 10 minutes

INGREDIENTS

Chicken	800 gms / 28 oz	Ginger	60 gms / 2 oz
Pineapple	240 gms / 9 oz	Garlic	20 gms
Capsicum	120 gms / 4 oz	Oil	¾ cup / 150 ml / 5 fl oz
Onions	60 gms / 2 oz	Oyster sauce	4 tsp / 20 ml
Spring onions	40 gms / 1¼ oz	Fish sauce	4 tsp / 20 ml
Red chillies	6-8	Chicken stock	3 tbs / 45 ml / 1½ fl oz
Mushrooms	60 gms / 2 oz		

METHOD

- Cut the chicken into strips and blanch.
- Cut the pineapple, capsicum, onions, spring onions and red chillies into quarters. Slice the mushrooms, shred the ginger and chop the garlic.
- Heat oil in a wok, sauté chopped garlic, add the chicken along with the remaining ingredients and chicken stock.
- Toss well on high heat, reduce heat and cook till vegetables are tender.
- Remove from heat and serve hot, accompanied by steamed rice.

Panaeng Kai

Serves - 4

Chicken stir-fried in thick red curry

Preparation time: 15 minutes

Cooking time: 15 minutes

INGREDIENTS

Chicken	800 gms / 28 oz
Panaeng curry paste	5 tbs / 75 gms / 2½ oz
Coconut milk	1 cup / 200 ml / 7 fl oz
Basil	8-10 leaves
Kaffir leaves	5
Fish sauce	4 tbs / 60 ml / 2 fl oz
Red chillies	3
Green chillies	3

METHOD

- Cut the chicken into strips.
- Heat a pan, add the Panaeng curry paste, chicken strips and coconut milk. Cook for 4-5 minutes.
- Add basil, kaffir leaves, fish sauce, red chillies and green chillies, mix well and simmer for 10 minutes. (If required stir in chicken stock).
- Remove from heat and serve hot.

Kaeng Karee Kai

Serves - 4

Mildly spiced yellow curry with chicken

Preparation time: 15 minutes

Cooking time: 15 minutes

INGREDIENTS

Chicken	800 gms / 28 oz
Oil	¾ cup / 150 ml / 5 fl oz
Yellow curry paste	5 tbs / 80 gms / 2¾ oz
Onions	120 gms / 4 oz
Coconut milk	1 cup / 200 ml / 7 fl oz
Fish sauce	4 tbs / 60 ml / 2 fl oz
Sugar	2 tbs / 30 gms / 1 oz
Salt to taste	

METHOD

- Cut the chicken into strips.
- Heat oil in a pan, add yellow curry paste and onions, sauté for 2-3 minutes.
- Stir in the remaining ingredients and cook on low heat for 15 minutes. (If required add a little chicken stock.)
- Stir in salt to taste and remove from heat.
- Serve hot, accompanied by steamed rice.

Patani

Serves - 4

Stir-fried lamb with ginger and garlic

Preparation time: 20 minutes

Cooking time: 10 minutes

INGREDIENTS

Lamb	800 gms / 28 oz	Garlic	40 gms / 1¼ oz
Capsicum	80 gms / 2¾ oz	Oil	¾ cup / 150 ml / 5 fl oz
Onion	60 gms / 2 oz	Fish sauce	2 tsp / 10 ml
Red chillies	4-6	Oyster sauce	2 tsp / 10 ml
Spring onion	60 gms / 2 oz	Light soya sauce	1 tsp / 6 ml
Ginger	80 gms / 2¾ oz	Pepper	1 tsp / 5 gms

METHOD

- Cut the lamb into slices, blanch and keep aside.
- Cut the capsicum, onion, red chillies, spring onions into pieces.
- Shred ginger and chop garlic.
- Heat oil in a wok, add the garlic and sauté until light brown.
- Add the capsicum, onion, red chillies and spring onions along with ginger and sauté for a minute.
- Stir in fish sauce, oyster sauce, light soya sauce and pepper. Toss on high heat for 5 minutes.
- Remove from heat onto a serving dish and serve hot.

Kaeng Khreo Wan Nuea

Serves - 4

A spiced green curry with lamb

Preparation time: 15 minutes

Cooking time: 15 minutes

INGREDIENTS

Veal tenderloin	800 gms / 28 oz
Oil	¾ cup / 150 ml / 5 fl oz
Green curry paste (pg. i)	½ cup / 100 gms / 3½ oz
Pia aubergine	120 gms / 4 oz
Kaffir leaves	4-6
Red chillies	4
Basil leaves	6-8
Coconut milk	1 cup / 200 ml / 7 fl oz
Fish sauce	3 tbs / 45 ml / 1½ fl oz
Sugar	4 tsp / 20 gms
Salt to taste	

METHOD

- Cut the tenderloin into pieces.
- Heat oil in a pan, add green curry paste alongwith the sliced tenderloin and sauté for 2-3 minutes.
- Stir in the pia aubergine, kaffir leaves, red chillies, basil, coconut milk, fish sauce and sugar.
- Cook on low heat for 15 minutes. (If required add a little chicken stock.)
- Add salt to taste and serve hot, accompanied by steamed rice.

Pla Thod Krathieum Prik Thai

Serves - 4

Deep fried crispy pomfret

Preparation time: 15 minutes

Cooking time: 20 minutes

INGREDIENTS

Pomfret, whole	1 (350 gms) / 12 oz
Fish sauce	2 tbs / 30 ml / 1 fl oz
Garlic	10 gms
Cornflour	4 tbs / 60 gms / 2 oz
Oil for frying	
Red chillies	3
Kaffir leaves	3
Red curry paste	4 tbs / 60 gms / 2 oz
Oyster sauce	1 tbs / 15 ml
Sugar	1 tsp / 5 gms
Lemon juice	2 tbs / 30 ml / 1 fl oz
Green coriander	6-8 sprigs

METHOD

- Clean the pomfret, remove fins, cut the belly and make gashes.
- Marinate the pomfret with fish sauce and rub garlic.
- Dissolve cornflour in water and coat the pomfret with it. Deep fry in hot oil until crisp and golden brown. Remove and keep aside.
- Chop red chillies and kaffir leaves.
- Heat oil in a wok, add red curry paste alongwith red chillies, kaffir leaves, oyster sauce, sugar and lemon juice.
- Sauté on high heat for a few minutes.
- Place the pomfret on a serving platter and pour the prepared sauce on top. Garnish with sprigs of green coriander and serve hot.

Hor Mok Thalay

Serves - 4

A combination of seafood, coconut milk and curry paste steam baked in a coconut shell

Preparation time: 15 minutes

Cooking time: 25-30 minutes

INGREDIENTS

Tender coconut	2
Fish	150 gms / 5 oz
Prawns	150 gms / 5 oz
Squid	100 gms / 3½ oz
Red curry paste (pg. i)	¾ cup / 150 gms / 5 oz
Kaffir leaves	6-8
Lemon grass	40 gms / 1¼ oz
Galangal (Kha)	40 gms / 1¼ oz
Coconut milk	1 cup / 200 ml / 7 fl oz
Egg, whisked	2
Red chilies	3
Green coriander to garnish	
Basil leaves	6-8

METHOD

- Cut open the top of the tender coconut, remove the coconut milk and keep aside.
- Mix prawns along with squid, red curry paste, kaffir leaves, basil, lemon grass, galangal, coconut milk and red chillies.
- Fill the tender coconut with the prepared mixture and pour the whisked egg on top.
- Place the coconut in a tray and steam for about 25 minutes.
- Remove the coconut from the steamer, garnish with green coriander and serve hot, accompanied by steamed rice.

Kaeng Phet Koong

Serves - 4

A hot red curry with prawns

Preparation time: 20 minutes

Cooking time: 10 minutes

INGREDIENTS

Prawns	400 gms / 14 oz	Red curry paste (pg. i)	¾ cup / 150 gms / 5 oz
Bamboo shoot	60 gms / 2 oz	Kaffir leaves	6-8 sprigs
White pumpkin	40 gms / 1¼ oz	Basil leaves	6-8
Red chillies	4	Coconut milk	1 cup / 200 ml / 7 fl oz
Mushrooms	60 gms / 2 oz	Fish sauce	3 tbs / 45 ml / 1½ fl oz
Oil	4 tbs / 60 ml / 2 fl oz	Sugar	4 tsp / 20 gms

METHOD

- Clean and devein the prawns. Cut the bamboo shoots and blanch. Cut the white pumpkin and red chillies into quarters. Slice the mushrooms.
- Heat oil in a pan, add red curry paste, cook for 2-3 minutes. Add kaffir leaves along with all the vegetables, basil, coconut milk, fish sauce and sugar.
- Cook on low heat for 5-10 minutes.
- Remove from heat and serve hot, accompanied by steamed rice.

Khao Phad Phak

Serves - 4

Vegetable fried rice

Preparation time: 30 minutes

Cooking time: 20 minutes

INGREDIENTS

Steamed rice	600 gms / 22 oz	Cauliflower	80 gms / 2¾ oz
Cabbage	80 gms / 2¾ oz	Garlic, chopped	10 gms
Carrots	80 gms / 2¾ oz	Salt to taste	
Green peas	80 gms / 2¾ oz	Pepper to taste	
Mushrooms	80 gms / 2¾ oz	Oil	¾ cup / 150 ml / 5 fl oz
Broccoli	80 gms / 2¾ oz	Soya sauce	2 tsp / 10 ml

METHOD

- Cut the cabbage into dices and mushrooms into halves. Cut the broccoli and cauliflower into florets.
- Blanch the cabbage and mushrooms along with broccoli and cauliflower florets. Remove from heat and keep aside.
- Heat oil in a wok and sauté garlic. Stir in the remaining ingredients and toss on high heat for a few minutes.
- Remove from heat and serve hot.

Khao Phad Bai Krapaw Kai

Serves - 4

Chicken fried rice with basil leaves

Preparation time: 30 minutes

Cooking time: 15 minutes

INGREDIENTS

Steamed rice	600 gms / 22 oz	Basil leaves	20
Chicken strips	240 gms / 9 oz	Garlic	20 gms
Spring onions, cut into strips	240 gms / 9 oz	Oil	¾ cup / 150 ml / 5 fl oz
Red chillies, whole	4	Soya sauce	2 tsp /10 ml
Green chillies	4		

METHOD

- Chop the red chillies along with green chillies and garlic. Blanch the chicken strips and keep aside.
- Heat oil in a wok and sauté the chopped red chillies, green chillies and garlic.
- Add the blanched chicken strips and sauté. Stir in the remaining ingredients and toss well.
- Serve hot, garnished with strips of spring onion.

Khao Phad Sapparod

Serves - 4

Fried rice with shredded chicken and pineapple

Preparation time: 10 minutes

Cooking time: 10 minutes

INGREDIENTS

Steamed rice	600 gms / 22 oz
Chicken	120 gms / 4 oz
Green peas	120 gms / 4 oz
Pineapple	120 gms / 4 oz
Spring onions	60 gms / 2 oz
Oil	¾ cup / 150 ml / 5 fl oz
Garlic	20 gms
Raisins	2 tbs / 30 gms / 1 oz
Soya sauce	2 tsp / 10 ml
Salt to taste	
Pepper to taste	
Sugar a pinch	
Cashew nuts, crushed	40 gms / 1¼ oz

METHOD

- Blanch the chicken and chop the pineapple and spring onions.
- Heat oil in a wok, add garlic and sauté for few minutes. Mix in green peas, pineapple, chicken, raisins and toss for a while.
- Stir in the steamed rice, soya sauce, salt, pepper and sugar. Mix well.
- Remove from heat and serve hot, garnished with crushed cashewnuts.

Guey Tiew Phat Khee Mao

Serves - 4

Stir-fried noodles

Preparation time: 40 minutes

Cooking time: 15 minutes

INGREDIENTS

Rice noodles	500 gms / 1.1 lb	Lemon grass	30 gms / 1 oz
Chicken, julienned	120 gms / 4 oz	Galangal (Kha)	30 gms / 1 oz
Spring onions, cut into strips	180 gms / 6 oz	Fish sauce	2 tbs / 30 ml / 1 fl oz
Garlic	40 gms / 1¼ oz	Oyster sauce	4 tsp / 20 ml
Green chillies	6	Soya sauce	1 tsp / 6 ml
Basil leaves	20-30	Oil	¾ cup / 150 ml / 5 fl oz

METHOD

- Soak the rice noodles in water for 25 minutes. Drain and keep aside.
- Blanch the julienned chicken and keep aside.
- Chop garlic, green chillies, basil leaves, lemon grass and galangal.
- In a wok, heat oil and add the chopped garlic, green chillies, lemon grass and galangal. Sauté for a few minutes and add chicken juliennes. Sauté further for a few seconds and stir in the remaining ingredients.
- Mix well and toss on high heat for a few seconds. Remove and serve hot.

Phad Thai

Serves - 4

Traditionally famous Thai noodles

Preparation time: 30 minutes

Cooking time: 20 minutes

INGREDIENTS

Phad thai noodles	400 gms / 14 oz
Water as required	
Tofu	120 gms / 4 oz
Oil	¾ cup / 150 ml / 5 fl oz + for frying
Preserved vegetables	45 gms / 1½ oz
Prawns	10
Garlic cloves	25 gms
Red chillies, pounded	2 tsp / 10 gms
Lemon juice	4 tbs / 60 ml /2 fl oz
Tamarind extract	2 tbs / 30 ml / 1 fl oz
Sugar	4 tsp / 20 gms
Fish sauce	2 tbs / 30 ml 1 fl oz
Tomato ketchup	4 tbs / 60 ml / 2 fl oz
Peanuts	50 gms / 1¾ oz
Lemon wedges to garnish	
Beansprouts	50 gms / 1¾ oz

METHOD

- Soak the noodles in water for half an hour, drain and keep aside.
- Cut tofu into 1-inch batons and deep fry in hot oil. Chop the preserved vegetables.
- Clean and blanch the prawns. Heat oil (2 tbs) in a wok, add the noodles along with the remaining ingredients except crushed peanuts and toss well on high heat.
- Remove from heat and add the peanuts, return to heat and toss well.
- Serve hot, garnished with lemon wedges and beansprouts.

Yam Woon Sen

Serves - 4

Mildly spiced vermicelli and shrimp salad

Preparation time: 20 minutes

Cooking time: 10 minutes

INGREDIENTS

Rice vermicelli	400 gms / 14 oz	Carrots	80 gms / 2¾ oz
Water as required		Ginger	80 gms / 2¾ oz
Onions	120 gms / 4 oz	Celery	60 gms / 2 oz
Spring onions	120 gms / 4 oz	Oil	4 tbs / 60 ml / 2 fl oz
Red chillies	4	Fish sauce to taste	
Green chillies	4	Lemon juice	3 tbs / 45 ml / 1½ fl oz
Mushrooms	120 gms / 4 oz	Sugar	3½ tbs / 60 gms / 2 oz
Prawns	240 gms / 9 oz	Water	1¼ cups / 240 ml / 8 fl oz

METHOD

- Soak the rice vermicelli in water for 15 minutes. Drain and keep aside.
- Cut the onions, spring onions, red chillies, green chillies and mushrooms into slices.
- Clean and cut the prawns into halves.
- Cut the carrot, ginger and celery into juliennes.
- Heat oil in a pan, add all the ingredients along with water (4 tbs).
- Stir in the fish sauce, lemon juice and sugar. Cook for 2 minutes or until the vegetables are tender.
- Remove from heat and serve.

Baa Mee Phad Thalay

Serves - 4

Stir-fried noodles with seafood

Preparation time: 20 minutes

Cooking time: 15 minutes

INGREDIENTS

Egg noodles	500 gms / 1.1 lb	Pepper	a pinch or two
Squids	100 gms / 3½ oz	Fish Sauce	2 tsp / 10 ml
Prawns	100 gms / 3½ oz	Soya Sauce	1 tsp / 5 ml
Sea fish	100 gms / 3½ oz	Garlic cloves, chopped	3
Mushrooms	120 gms / 4 oz	Oil	¾ cup / 150 ml / 5 fl oz
Spring onions, chopped	60 gms / 2 oz	Oyster sauce	1 tsp / 5 ml

METHOD

- Boil noodles in sufficient water. Drain and allow to cool.
- Add a little oil to the noodles to prevent them from sticking.
- Clean the squids, prawns and sea fish. Cut into dices and blanch.
- Heat oil in a wok, add garlic and saute for a few seconds.
- Add the blanched squids, prawns and sea fish along with mushrooms and noodles. Toss well.
- Mix in pepper, fish sauce, soya sauce, oyster sauce and toss on high heat for a few minutes.
- Remove from heat and add spring onions. Serve hot.

Baa Mee Phad Phak

Serves - 4

Stir-fried noodles with vegetables

Preparation time: 30 minutes

Cooking time: 10 minutes

INGREDIENTS

Egg noodles	500 gms / 1.1 lb	Salt to taste	
Carrots	120 gms / 4 oz	Pepper to taste	
Cauliflower	120 gms / 4 oz	Soya sauce	2 tsp / 10 ml
Mushrooms	120 gms / 4 oz	Garlic, chopped	12 gms
Babycorn	120 gms / 4 oz	Oil	¾ cups / 150 ml / 5 fl oz
Spring onions, chopped	60 gms / 2 oz	Oyster sauce	2 tsp / 10 ml

METHOD

- Boil noodles in sufficient water. Drain and allow to cool. Add a little oil to the noodles to prevent them from sticking.
- Cut the carrots and mushrooms into slices, cauliflower into florets and babycorn into diamonds.
- Blanch all the vegetables and keep aside.
- Heat oil in a wok, sauté garlic and add all the vegetables and noodles. Toss well.
- Mix in salt, pepper, soya sauce, oyster sauce and toss in high heat.
- Remove from heat and mix in spring onions. Serve hot.

Met Khonon

Serves - 4

Lentil dumplings cooked in sugar syrup

Preparation time: 20 minutes

Cooking time: 30 minutes

INGREDIENTS

Palm sugar	2 cups / 400 gms / 14 oz
Eggs (yolk only)	10
Lentils	400 gms / 14 oz
Sugar syrup	4 cups / 800 ml / 28 fl oz
Pandanus essence	4 drops
Coconut milk	1¼ cups / 240 ml / 8 fl oz
Water	4 cups / 800 ml / 28 fl oz

METHOD

- Boil the lentils along with palm sugar and water till the lentils are tender.
- Blend the lentlis to a thick puree and mix in pandanus essence.
- Divide into equal portions and shape into oval dumplings.
- Make a mixture of egg yolk and coconut milk and dip the dumplings in it for a few minutes. Remove and keep aside.
- Heat sugar syrup and poach the dumplings in it for about 5-6 minutes.
- Remove from the sugar syrup and serve warm.

Lot Chong

Serves - 4

Pandanus flavoured thick noodles served with coconut milk and crushed ice

Preparation time: 2 hours

Cooking time: 30 minutes

INGREDIENTS

Hulled mungbeans	240 gms / 9 oz
Tapioca flour	400 gms / 14 oz
Water, boiled	½ cup / 150 ml / 5 fl oz
Pandanus essence	2-3 drops
Green food colour	4 drops
Jasmine water	½ cup / 100 ml / 3½ fl oz
Sugar	2 cups / 400 gms / 14 oz
Coconut milk	2 cups / 400 gms / 14 oz

METHOD

- Soak the mungbeans in water for 1½ hours. Boil and mash to a smooth paste.
- Mix the washed mungbeans with tapioca flour. Add the boiling water along with the pandanus juice and green food colour.
- Allow to cool and knead into a soft, sticky dough. Roll the dough into a thin sheet and cut into strands.
- In a pan, boil water and put the strands in it. When they float, remove and put in a pan of cold water for a few minutes.
- Meanwhile, for the coconut syrup, boil sugar and jasmine water for 5 minutes, allow to cool and add coconut milk. Remove and keep aside.
- Drain the mungbean strands and pour into the prepared coconut syrup.
- Serve with ice.

Aisa Khrim Mapraw

Serves - 4

Homemade coconut ice cream

Preparation time: 15 minutes + time for freezing

Cooking time: 20 minutes

INGREDIENTS

Coconut powder, roasted	120 gms / 4 oz	Milk powder	1 cup / 240 gms / 9 oz
Milk	1 litre / 32 fl oz	Sugar	2 cups / 400 gms / 14 oz
Cream	400 gms / 14 oz	Eggs, yolk	6

METHOD

- Mix milk along with cream, milk powder, sugar and egg yolks. Pour into a thick bottomed pan and cook on low heat, stirring constantly till it begins to thicken.
- Remove from heat and allow to cool.
- Pour the mixture in an ice cream maker.
- When ready mix in coconut powder. Remove from the ice cream maker and freeze. Serve in ice cream glasses.